Digital Photographic Manipulation

Linda W. Wood
Marilyn Stockton

 The Art Institute of Atlanta®

ACQUISITIONS EDITOR   Kas Salazar
COVER DESIGN   Linda W. Wood

This custom textbook includes materials submitted by the Authors for publication by John Wiley & Sons, Inc. The material has not been edited by Wiley and the Authors are solely responsible for its content.

Photographs, illustrations, design: Linda W. Wood
Editing and Introduction: Marilyn Stockton

This textbook was prepared in conjunction with a course offered at The Art Institute of Atlanta, 6600 Peachtree Dunwoody Road, 100 Embassy Row, Atlanta, Georgia 30328-1635, (770)394-8300, (800)275-4242. www.aia.artinstitutes.edu.

To order books or for customer service please call 1-800-CALL WILEY (255-5945).

ISBN 0-471-99821-4

Printed in the United States of America

10 9 8 7 6 5 4 3 2 1

TABLE OF CONTENTS

INTRODUCTION

Image manipulation was once the preserve of experts with cameras and photographic chemicals, but the digital explosion of the last two decades has made a vast array of techniques available to anyone with a computer and the proper software. Professions such as photographic imaging, graphic design, web design, advertising, and animation have required expertise in digital image manipulation for a least a decade. Other fields such as interior design, video, and audio are beginning to give preference in hiring to candidates who also have the capability of creating and manipulating digital images for presentation purposes and for the production of collateral print materials in a professional manner.

Along with the technology explosion, a vast amount of literature has been produced to introduce students and other interested parties to the wonders of digital image manipulation and especially to the Adobe Photoshop® software that is now marketed as a part of the software suite Adobe CS2®. So why this book when there are so many other good ones out there? Because we were unable to find a text that covered what we needed at The Art Institute of Atlanta in the way that we have decided is the most effective way to present the material. Students learn software applications best by doing them, and thus based on many years experience in teaching digital image manipulation, we have developed a series of eight tutorials designed to introduce students to many of the applications of Adobe Photoshop®.

These tutorials included detailed, step-by-step instructions and are designed to be completed by the student with only occasional help from an instructor. Thus each student can work at his or her own pace. Moreover, this process forces students to read and actually pay attention to instructions. Another advantage is that the text gives students a place to refer in the future when they can't quite remember how something works.

However, the tutorials work best when they are supplemented with background material from a qualified teacher and when they are reinforced with outside-of-class projects that build on the skills developed in the tutorials. Also it should be emphasized that the tutorials build on each other in a linear fashion, which makes skipping a tutorial (or a class) a problem, and students should be periodically tested on the material to ensure that they are learning it.

TUTORIALS

Photoshop Tutorial
Workshop 1 – Image Editing / Composite Image

OBJECTIVE: After completing this Workshop Tutorial, you will be able to edit photographs as well as create composite images using Adobe Photoshop®. You will also be introduced to using selection tools and filters in this Workshop Tutorial.

Create a folder on your desktop and name it "Photoshop Tutorial 1." Save all of your files during the Workshop to this folder. At the end of this tutorial, drag your desktop folder to your USB Flash Drive or burn on a CD.

DRAG TO YOUR DESKTOP FOLDER FROM YOUR CD: Photoshop Tutorial 1 Images

1. Open Adobe Photoshop®.

2. Open Yellow Flowers.jpg

3. HOLD the Command Key on your Keyboard (or Control Key on the PC) plus the 0 (zero) key, to enlarge the document to "Fit on Screen" This command expands the document larger to fit better within your computer monitor. You can use your Navigator palette (on the right side of your screen) to see where you are on your document as well as zoom in and zoom out. You can also use the **Zoom Tool** to enlarge your view and hold the Option key + the Zoom Tool to zoom out.

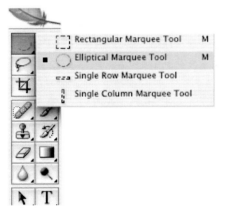

4. Using your Toolbox (floating on the left side of your screen), click your mouse and hold on the Rectangular Marquee to select the **Elliptical Marquee**.

5. Hold down the Shift Key (the Shift Key will draw a perfect circle) and draw a circle over the center of the large yellow flower on the left side of the photo using the Elliptical Marquee and your mouse. The Elliptical Marquee is a selection tool used in Adobe Photoshop®. There are 4 selection Marquees: Rectangular, Elliptical, Single Row and Single Column. You will see flashing dashed lines after you let go of the mouse. These flashing dashed lines show you what you have selected. In order to affect an image or a portion of the image, the area needs to be selected.

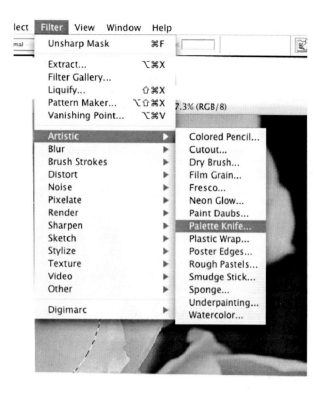

6. Go under the **Filter** menu and select **Artistic > Palette Knife**. Pull the STROKE size to 35. Click OK.

Notice that only what is inside of the selected circle is affected.

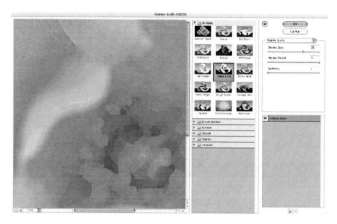

7. Go under the **Select** menu > **Inverse**. Now everything but the circle is selected. You will see the flashing dashed lines around the perimeter of the image.

8. Go back under the Filter menu and choose **Filter > Brush Stroke > Spatter**.

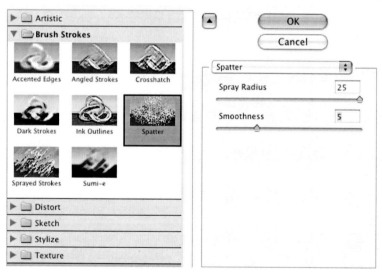

9. Drag the **Spray Radius** slider up to **25** and leave the smoothness at **5**.

10. Click OK.

11. **Select > Deselect**.

12. Go under the **File** menu > **Save As > Filtered Flowers.jpg**. This will save the new file into your desktop folder.

13. You are finished with this document. Close the document by holding the **Command Key + W** (Mac) OR the Control Key + W for the PC.

Composite Photos

Next, you will create a composite photo. A composite photo is one made up of more than one photograph. When creating composite photos, you will be using Layers and the Layers Palette.

14. Open Beach.jpg from your desktop folder by either using the **File > Open** command or using **File > Browse** to open Adobe Bridge® and navigate to your desktop folder.

15. **Command + 0** (Zero) or Control + 0 (Zero) for the PC to Fit on Screen.

16. **File > Open** or **File > Browse** and open up Clown.jpg from your desktop folder.

17. Using your **Move Tool** (the top right tool in your Toolbox), arrange the two so that you can see both documents open at the same time on your computer screen.

18. Make sure the Layers Palette is visible on the right side of your screen.

19. Using your mouse, drag the "Background" layer from the Layers Palette in the Clown document and drop into the Beach document window.

20. Now the Clown should be in the Beach document. You may close the original Clown file.

21. In the Layers palette in the Beach document, you should see 2 layers: Background (which is the Beach) and Layer 1 (which is the Clown).

22. Double-click on the **WORD** "Layer 1" to get a text box that will allow you to rename Layer 1 as "Clown."

23. Double click on the "Background" layer and name it "Beach." Layer 0 Dialog Box appears, type in "Beach."

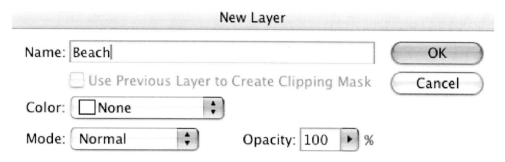

24. **FILE > Save As > Beach Composite.psd (make sure you select PHOTOSHOP as the type of file).**

25. The Clown is too large and will need to be scaled down. In order to activate the Clown layer, click once on the Clown layer. You must actually click on the layer in the Layers Palette to affect that layer (to move and transform the objects on the layer). You may need to use the **MOVE TOOL** to center the clown in the Beach composite photo.

26. Go under the **Edit** menu > **Transform** > **Scale**.

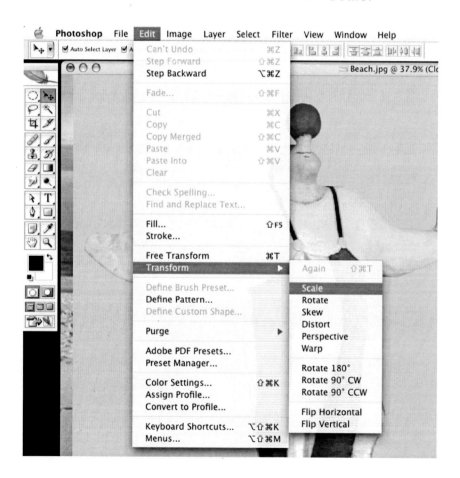

27. The Clown layer may be too large to see the handles of the transformation box. In the **Navigator Palette**, double-click on the zoom percentage and type in **20** for the **zoom percentage** and press the Enter/Return key on your keyboard.

28. Now that you can see the transformation box in its entirety, you need to hold the **Shift** key (to scale proportionately) and take the top right corner of the Clown and pull inwards to scale the Clown smaller. You want to make it appear as if the Clown is in the foreground of the photograph.

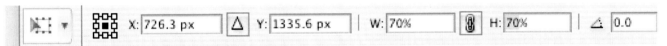

Notice that the width and height in percentage numbers are scaling in the **Options Bar** at the top of your screen as you are scaling the Clown down in size. You may also type in the % in the Options Bar if you need to have an accurate percentage. You may type in 70% here in the width and height % fields in the Options Bar. You want to scale the clown down to about 70% of its original size.

29. Once the Clown is scaled down to about 70% of its original size, hit the **RETURN/ENTER** key to make the transformation take effect.

Now you will use the **LASSO TOOL** to select the clown. The **LASSO TOOL** is one of 3 tools in the Lasso flyout, including the Polygon Lasso and the Magnetic Lasso.

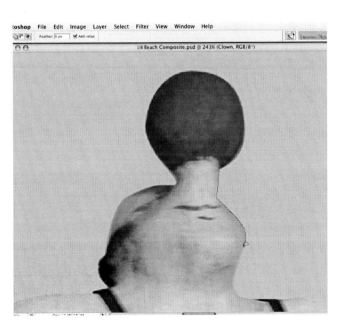

30. Using the **Lasso Tool,** press the mouse and trace the Clown. Take your time and trace slowly. You cannot let go of the mouse, otherwise the selection will not be accurate. If you accidentally let go of the mouse, hold down the Command Key (Control Key for the PC) and hit the "D" key on your keyboard to deselect. You will need to start the tracing over if you deselect. Using the Lasso Tool does take some practice. The Lasso Tool will show a circle when the selection is ready to close. You will see the flashing dashed lines of the selection once the selection has been made.

31. You will make a copy of the clown by selecting **EDIT > COPY**.

32. **EDIT > PASTE**.

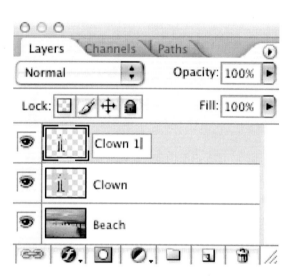

33. You have made another layer. Any time that you use the Paste command, another layer is made (Layer 1). **Double-click Layer 1 in the Layers Palette and name it "Clown 1."**

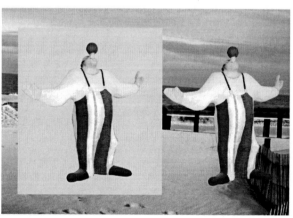

34. Using the Move Tool, drag the new clown to the right so that the two clowns are not overlapping. Your composite should look similar to the image on the left.

35. **File > Save.**

Taking a Snapshot

Adobe Photoshop© includes the ability to step backwards through your steps by using the History Palette. By default, the History Palette allows 20 undo's. This default may be changed under the Preferences option under the word "Photoshop" on the Mac and under the Edit menu on the PC. However there are some times where you might like the option of going back to a certain state of the image manipulation where you were about 40 steps ago. Since the History Palette only offers 20 undo's by default, you will want to periodically take a Snapshot. A Snapshot will take you back the state where you took the Snapshot. So, if you work through 40 more steps and you do not like the results, you can click on the Snapshot and revert back to that state.

36. In the History Palette, click on the Snapshot icon at the bottom of the palette.

37. You have created a Snapshot that you can go back to if needed at a later time. However, once you have saved and closed the file, the Snapshots are not stored or saved with the file. They are gone. If you are working on a file for a long time, you will have several Snapshots.

38. You will need to make the Clown 1 smaller. Make sure the Clown 1 layer is activated. **Edit > Transform > Scale**. Holding the Shift Key, drag the bottom right corner inwards to scale. Look in the Options Bar to make sure you are scaling this clown to 80% in width and height.

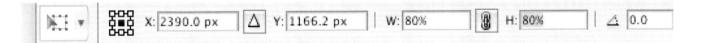

39. Press the **Return/Enter Key** to make the transformation take effect.

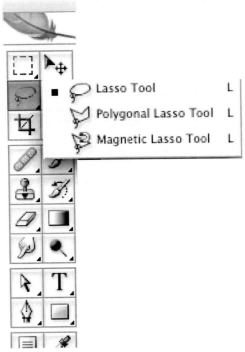

40. Now you will use another selection tool - the **Magnetic Lasso**  . The Magnetic Lasso is located underneath the Lasso Tool. You must click and hold on the Lasso Tool in the Toolbox and to select the Magnetic Lasso.

41. The **Magnetic Lasso** selects by color and tonal pixel values, so it "snaps" to the edge of the object you are tracing. You must go slowly while tracing. You need only to click your mouse to create a starting point. After that, you will glide around the edge of the shape or object to create your selection, only clicking the mouse button to change direction. **Using the Magnetic Lasso, trace the original clown**. You will again see a small circle form when your selection is ready to close. Click **once** to close the selection.

42. **Layer Via Copy** - Go under the LAYER MENU to **Layer > New > Layer Via Copy** (or use the keyboard shortcut: Cmd + J for the Mac or Ctrl + J for the PC).

If you want to copy and paste an object at the same time, you should use the Layer Via Copy command. It will create a new layer with the object you copied on that new layer.

43. Using the **Move Tool** drag the new clown off of the original clown.

44. Go under **Edit > Free Transform** to scale the new clown down. Hold the Shift Key while dragging the bottom right corner inwards. Watching the Options Bar, scale the clown down to **60%**.

45. Press the **Return/Enter Key** to make the transformation take effect.

46. Double-click the **WORD** Layer 1 in the Layers palette to rename the Layer **Clown 2**.

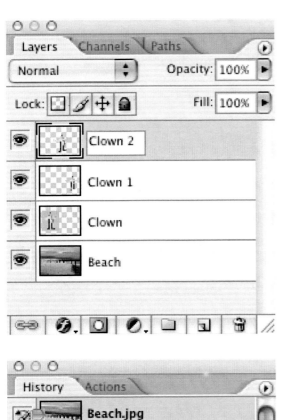

You now should have 4 Layers in the Layers Palette.

47. In the History Palette, **create another Snapshot** by clicking on the Snapshot icon 📷 .

48. You should now have 3 Snapshots in your History Palette. Click on Beach.jpg in the History Palette and see that your composite image reverts back to that state.

49. Click on the Beach Composite Snapshot. The image reverts back to the original image.

50. **Click back on Snapshot 2** and your image returns to the current state.

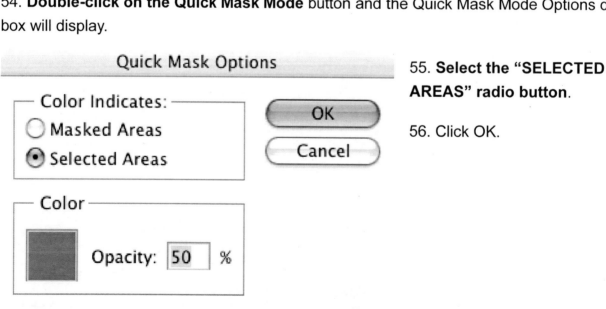

51. **File > Save**.

Quick Mask

The **Quick Mask** is a way to "paint" your selection. Some use the Quick Mask to touch up selections that they have made using other selection tools. At time, a shape may lend itself to using a paint brush instead of a rectangle or lasso to select. The Quick Mask creates a semi-transparent mask that covers the areas you paint with the Brush or Pencil Tool. The mask applies the semi-transparent color to show the areas you are selecting. The default is to select the "Masked Areas." However, you will change the Quick Mask Options and select the "Selected Areas" instead.

52. Activate the original Clown layer by clicking on it with your mouse in the Layers Palette. **Press the "D" Key** on the Keyboard to make sure you have the Default Colors in the Toolbox. Black should be the Foreground Color and White the Background color. In the Quick Mask Mode, the color black acts as the "paint" and the color white acts as the "eraser."

53. The **Quick Mask Mode** is located at the bottom right side of your Toolbox.

54. **Double-click on the Quick Mask Mode** button and the Quick Mask Mode Options dialog box will display.

55. **Select the "SELECTED AREAS" radio button**.

56. Click OK.

57. Select the **Brush Tool** 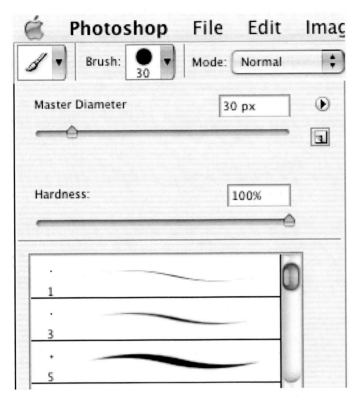 in your Toolbox.

58. In your **Options Bar, click and hold the arrow next to the Brush size icon to get the Brush Options.**

59. **Select a #30 bush** by typing in 30 in the Master Diameter area.

60. Type in **100% in the Hardness area**.

61. Hit the Return/Enter Key to make the Brush Options box disappear.

62. "Paint" the original Clown. Notice that the "color" is red. You are not really painting a color, you are creating a selection by using the Brush Tool. Try to stay within the lines of the Clown and fill the Clown in completely. You may need to increase the size of the Brush when you fill in the Quick Mask after outlining the Clown.

You have a 50% red color so that you can see what you are selecting. If you make a mistake using the Quick Mask, hit the "X" Key on your Keyboard to switch foreground and background colors to use white to clean up the mistake (you also could hit the **SWITCH ARROW** above the foreground/background swatch on the Toolbox.)

Foreground/Background Switch Arrow

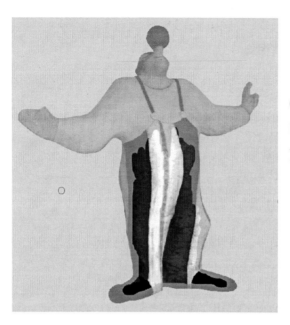

63. As you begin to use the Brush Tool with the Quick Mask, you will see the "paint" masking out the area you want selected.

64. Once the Clown has been "painted," click on the **Standard Mode** button (to the left of the Quick Mask button you clicked on previously). The Quick Mask goes away and the "paint" turns into a selection (the flashing dashed lines).

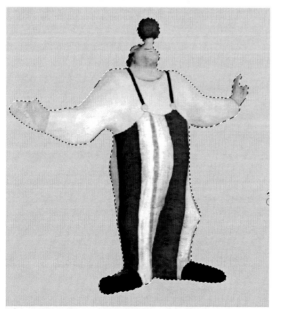

65. **Command +J (for the Mac) OR Control + J (for the PC) to copy and paste the Clown to a new layer**. Move the new Clown with the **MOVE TOOL** off of the original Clown. You now should have 5 layers.

66. **File > Save**.

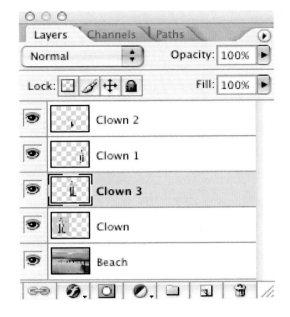

67. Double-click the **WORD** Layer 1 and change the name to **Clown 3**.

68. To scale the Clown 3 down, **Edit > Transform > Scale**.

69. Holding the **Shift Key**, drag the bottom right corner inwards until the width and height in the Options Bar states **45%**.

70. Press the **Return/Enter Key** to make the transformation take effect.

71. File > Save.

72. Select your Move Tool .

73. In the Layers Palette, click on the **original Clown layer.**

74. Drag the original Clown layer to the top of the Layers stack.

Now you are ready to get rid of the yellow square around the original Clown layer.

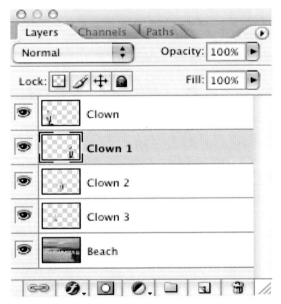

75. Using the **Magic Wand Tool** , click on the yellow square behind the original Clown. The yellow background is selected.

76. Press the **Delete Key.**

77. Hold the Command Key (Control Key for the PC) and hit the "D" Key to **Deselect**. This is the keyboard shortcut.

78. **File > Save**.

79. Your LAYERS should look like the image of the LAYERS PALETTE on the left.

80. Click on the top layer in your layers palette.

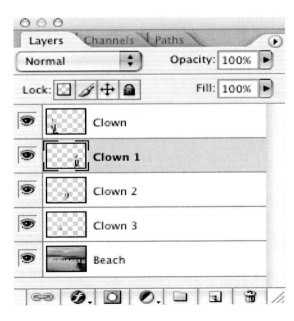

81. Using the **Move Tool**, select the **"Auto Select Layer"** option in the Options Bar. This option allows you to automatically select the layer in the Layers Palette when you select the object in the composite image. This could be very helpful when rearranging your objects in the composite but also it may become a hindrance. You can always deselect the Auto Select Layer option.

82. Click on the largest Clown in the composite**.**

83. Notice that the Clown layer is automatically selected.

84. Move the large clown to the bottom left of the image to make it appear as if it is in the foreground of the photo.

85. Move the other clowns one at a time to arrange the clowns in positions similar to the sample below. The larger clowns should be in the foreground and the smaller clowns in the background to give some perspective.

86. Click on Clown 3 (the smallest clown in the back).

87. **Edit > Transform > Flip Horizontal.** This command will flip the clown to face the left instead of the right.

88. Click on **Clown 1** on the right side of the image (the second largest clown).

89. **Edit > Transform > Flip Horizontal.**

90. Now your composite image should look similar to this.

91. **File > Save.**

Creating Shadows

92. Select the Move Tool.

93. In the **Options Bar, deselect the "Auto Select Layer"** option.

94. Click on the Clown 2 layer in the Layers Palette.

95. Command + J (or Control + J for the PC).

96. Drag the new Clown 2 Copy layer **below** the Clown 2 layer in the Layers Palette.

97. Double-click on the **WORD** Clown 2 Copy to rename the Layer to **Clown 2 Shadow**.

98. **Edit > Transform > DISTORT**. This will allow you to distort the layer to appear as if the clown is lying down.

99. Drag the middle handle of the transformation box down and out to the left of the Clown 2.

100. Adjust the transformation so that the feet of the shadow and the feet of the Clown 2 match as in the image below. **Press the RETURN / ENTER Key** to make the transformation take effect.

Your transformation should look similar to the image below.

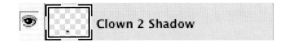 Clown 2 Shadow

101. Press the **Return/Enter Key** to make the transformation take effect.

102. Hold down the **Command Key (the Control Key for the PC) and click on the LAYER THUMBNAIL** of the Clown 2 Shadow layer in the Layers Palette. The "thumbnail" is the small square on the left side of the layer with an image of the layer inside. **This will select the entire layer. The Clown 2 Shadow is selected.**

103. Press the **DELETE** Key. The image inside of the selection is now deleted.

104. The selection needs to be softened. Go under the **Select Menu > Feather**. This will soften the edges of the selection.

105. Enter **20 in the Feather Radius** box in the dialog box that appears. **Click OK.**

106. This gives an extreme feather which will be useful for shadows.

107. The selection now appears rounded.

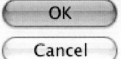

Feather Selection

Feather Radius: 20 pixels

OK

Cancel

108. **SELECT > INVERSE**. This will allow you to **VIGNETTE** (create a soft framing effect).

109. Press the **DELETE Key**.

110. **SELECT > INVERSE** (again).

111. File > Save.

112. Select the **Gradient Tool**  in the Toolbox.

113. In the **Options Bar, drag the OPACITY % to 40**.

114. Using the **Gradient Tool**, press and hold your mouse and drag a gradient from the feet of the Clown 2 towards the head of the shadow.

115. Your shadow should look similar to the image on the left.

116. **DESELECT**.

You will repeat this process of creating shadows for the Clown 1 layer and the Clown 3 layer.

117. Click on the Clown 1 layer in the Layers Palette to activate it.

118. Command + J (or Control + J for the PC).

119. Drag the new Clown 1 Copy layer **below** the Clown 1 layer in the Layers Palette.

120. Double-click on the **WORD** Clown 1 Copy to rename the Layer to **Clown 1 Shadow**.

121. **Edit > Transform > DISTORT**. This will allow you to distort the layer to appear as if the clown is lying down.

122. Drag the middle handle of the transformation box down and out to the left of the Clown 2.

123. Adjust the transformation so that the feet of the shadow and the feet of the Clown 2 match as in the image below. **Press the RETURN / ENTER Key** to make the transformation take effect.

Your transformation box should look similar to the image below.

124. Hold down the **Command Key (the Control Key for the PC) and click on the LAYER THUMBNAIL** of the Clown 1 Shadow layer in the Layers Palette to load the layer as a selection.

125. Press the **DELETE** Key. The image inside of the selection is now deleted.

Feather Selection

Feather Radius: 20   pixels

OK

Cancel

126. **Select Menu > Feather**. This will soften the edges of the selection.

127. Enter **20 in the Feather Radius** box in the dialog box that appears. **Click OK**.

128. **SELECT > INVERSE**.

129. Press the **DELETE Key**.

130. **SELECT > INVERSE** (again).

131. **File > Save**.

132. Select the **GRADIENT TOOL**  in the Toolbox.

133. In the **Options Bar, make sure the OPACITY % is still 40%**.

134. Using the **GRADIENT TOOL**, press and hold your mouse and drag a gradient from the feet of the Clown 1 towards the head of the shadow.

135. Your shadow should look similar to the image below.

136. **DESELECT**.

137. Click on the Clown 3 layer in the Layers Palette to activate it.

138. Command + J (or Control + J for the PC).

139. Drag the new Clown 3 Copy layer **below** the Clown 3 layer in the Layers Palette.

140. Double-click on the **WORD** Clown 3 Copy to rename the Layer to **Clown 3 Shadow**.

141. **Edit > Transform > DISTORT**. This will allow you to distort the layer to appear as if the clown is lying down.

142. Drag the middle handle of the transformation box down and out to the left of the Clown 3.

143. Adjust the transformation so that the feet of the shadow and the feet of the Clown 3 match as in the image below. **Press the RETURN / ENTER Key** to make the transformation take effect.

144. Hold down the **Command Key (the Control Key for the PC) and click on the LAYER THUMBNAIL** of the Clown 3 Shadow layer in the Layers Palette to load the layer as a selection.

145. Press the **DELETE** Key. The image inside of the selection is now deleted.

146. **Select Menu > Feather**.

Feather Selection

Feather Radius: `20` pixels

OK

Cancel

147. Enter **20 in the Feather Radius** box in the dialog box that appears. **Click OK**.

148. **SELECT > INVERSE**.

149. Press the **DELETE Key**.

150. **File > Save**.

151. **SELECT > INVERSE** (again).

152. Select the **Gradient Tool** in the Toolbox.

153. In the **Options Bar, make sure the OPACITY % is still 40%**.

154. Using the **Gradient Tool**, press and hold your mouse and drag a gradient from the feet of the Clown 3 towards the head of the shadow.

155. **Deselect**.

Your shadow and finished composite should look similar to the image below.

Beach Composite.psd @ 20% (Clown 3 copy, RGB/8*)

20%   Doc: 17.2M/39.6M

156. File > Save.

You may close the document.

You have finished this Workshop Tutorial.

Remember to drag your desktop folder to your USB Flash Drive or burn on a CD.

Workshop 2 – Selections and Alpha Channels

OBJECTIVE: After completing this Workshop Tutorial, you will practice using different methods of selecting objects within an image in Adobe Photoshop®. You will be saving selections as Alpha Channels and loading those Alpha Channels as selections. Blending Modes will also be introduced.

Create a folder on your desktop and name it "Photoshop Tutorial 2." Save all of your files during the Workshop to this folder. At the end of this tutorial, drag your desktop folder to your USB Flash Drive or burn on a CD.

DRAG TO YOUR DESKTOP FOLDER FROM YOUR CD: Photoshop Tutorial 2 Images

1. Open Adobe Photoshop®.

2. Open Fish Jars.jpg

3. Command Key (Mac) or Control Key (PC) + 0 (zero) to Fit on Screen.

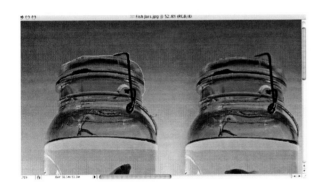

4. In the Toolbox, select the **Lasso Tool** .

5. Using the **LASSO TOOL**, trace around the first jar on the left, pressing down the mouse button as you trace. Hold the mouse button down the entire time as you trace. If you accidentally let go of the mouse, deselect and start the tracing over.

6. When you get back to the place where you began to trace, you will see a circle on the LASSO icon. You can let go of the mouse button when you see the circle icon and "dancing ants" (flashing dashed lines) will appear where you traced with the LASSO TOOL.

Cleaning Up Selections

7. To create a tight and accurate selection, use the **SHIFT KEY + the selection tool** if you need to add to the selection. If there are areas that need to be subtracted from the selection, use the **OPTION / ALT KEY + the selection tool** to take away unwanted areas.

Alpha Channels

An **ALPHA CHANNEL** is a selection you have saved to prevent having to select it over again. You will be able to use this selection anytime you need to without re-selecting - you will just need to LOAD the selection when needed. **ALPHA CHANNELS** are stored in the **CHANNELS PALETTE**.

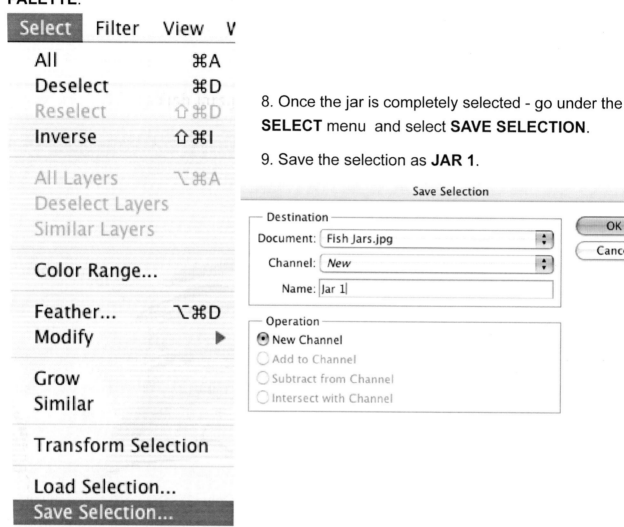

8. Once the jar is completely selected - go under the **SELECT** menu and select **SAVE SELECTION**.

9. Save the selection as **JAR 1**.

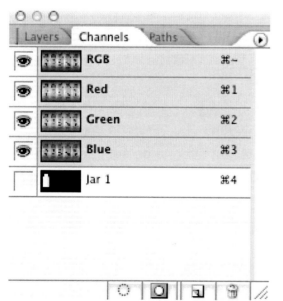

10. You've now created an **ALPHA CHANNEL**. Click on the Channels Palette tab next to the Layers tab and you can see the Alpha Channel mask.

The other Channels you see in the Channels Palette are color channels. The Color Channels display the color information in the file. This is a RGB image so you see the composite channel (RGB) at the top of the Channels Palette and the three channels: Red, Green and Blue channels displayed in gray scale to allow you make adjustments on the individual channels if necessary.

10. Now **Deselect** (Command + D for the Mac OR Control + D for the PC).

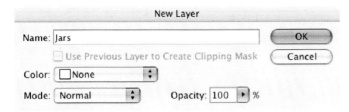

11. Click on the **LAYERS** tab to get the Layers Palette.

12. **Double-click the Background** layer and rename it "Jars."

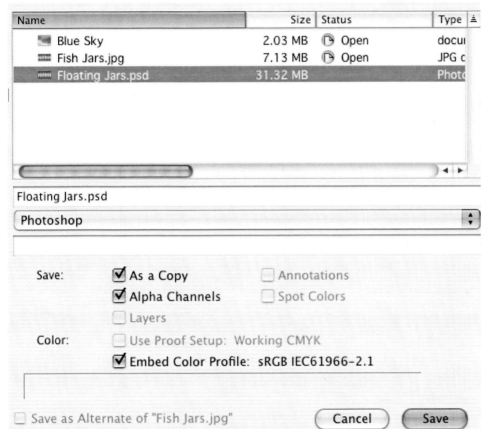

13. **File > Save As > Floating Jars. psd**. Make sure you save as a Photoshop document.

14. **Check the Save Alpha Channels box to make sure you are saving your Alpha Channels.**

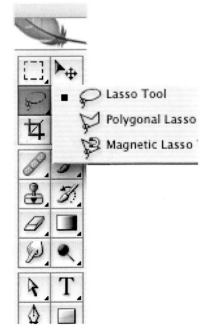

15. Click and hold on the LASSO tool to select the **MAGNETIC LASSO TOOL** .

The Magnetic Lasso Tool selects by color values. It "jumps" to snap to a shape determined by the colored values. This tool works great for selecting objects that have a contrast between the object you want to select and the background, but does not do as well when tonal values are similar. You can always snap points with the tool, especially to change direction. The jars are very similar in tonal values and color as the background.

16. In the **OPTIONS BAR, change the WIDTH to 1px**. This will not allow as many pixels to be considered when selecting with the tool, giving you a little more control when values are too similar. It allows the selection to be more accurate and precise.

17. Using the **MAGNETIC LASSO**, select the entire jar .

18. Use the Shift Key to add to the selection if you missed areas of the jar that needed to be included. Use the Option/Alt Key to subtract areas out of the selection. You might want to switch to the LASSO TOOL to clean up the selection.

19. **SELECT > SAVE SELECTION**.

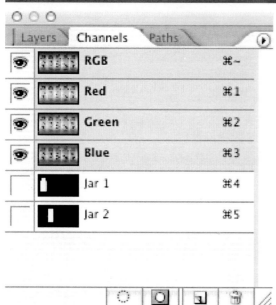

20. Save this new selection as **Jar 2**. You have now created a second Alpha Channel.

21. **File > Save**.

22. **DESELECT** (Command + D for the Mac OR Control + D for the PC).

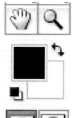

Default Colors

23. Press the **D key** to select **DEFAULT COLORS**. The Default colors will show in your Toolbox with Black as the Foreground Color and White as the Background Color.

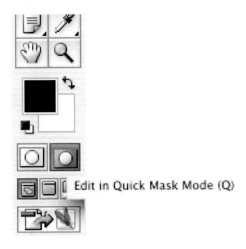

24. The next jar you choose to select, you will be using the **Quick Mask**.

25. When using the **Quick Mask Mode** (such as you did in Tutorial 1) to select an object, you are actually "painting" the object with a mask. When you are finished "painting" the selection, select the **Standard Mode Button** and the Quick Mask goes away and the object "painted" turns into a selection ("dancing ants").

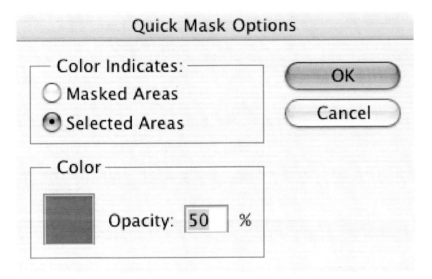

26. Double click on the **Quick Mask Mode** button - to open the Quick Mask Options dialog box.

27. Under the options menu dialog box - choose **SELECTED AREAS**.

28. Click OK.

30. Select the **ZOOM TOOL** in the Toolbox.

31. Click the ZOOM TOOL on the middle jar to zoom in.

32. Select the **BRUSH TOOL** .

33. Choose a **HARD BRUSH** in the **OPTIONS BAR. Make sure the OPACITY is set to 100%.**

34. In the **Quick Mask Mode**, paint the outline of the top of the jar.

35. Choose a **larger hard brush** (from the Options Bar to fill in the jar.

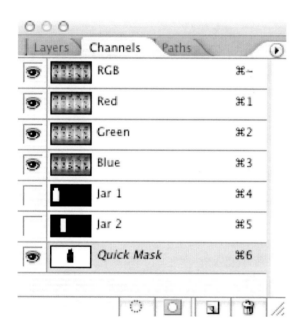

36. In the Channels Palette, you can see the temporary Quick Mask. Once you select the Standard Editing Mode, the mask will disappear in the Channels Palette.

37. After the entire jar is "painted" and filled in, click on the **Standard Mode button**. The Quick Mask disappears and the bottle is now selected.

38. Click on the **SELECT** menu and **SAVE SELECTION**.

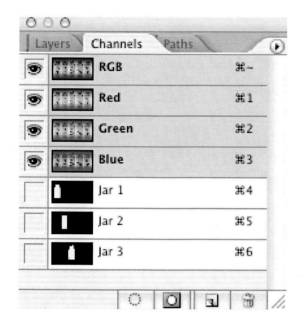

39. Save this selection as **Jar 3**. You now should have 3 Alpha Channels in your Channels Palette.

40. **DESELECT.**

41. **File > Save**.

42. You must now **select the 4th jar** by using either the Lasso Tool, the Magnetic Lasso Tool or the Quick Mask Mode.

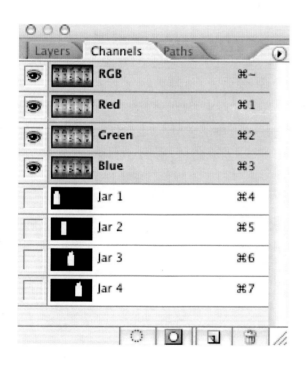

43. Once the 4th jar has been selected, **SELECT > SAVE SELECTION.** Save the selection as Jar 4.

44. **File > Save**.

45. **Select the 5th jar** by using either the Lasso Tool, the Magnetic Lasso Tool or the Quick Mask Mode.

46. Once the 5th jar has been selected, **SELECT > SAVE SELECTION**. Save the selection as Jar 5.

47. **File > Save**.

Loading an Alpha Channel as a Selection

48. In order to select the background behind the jars, you will select the jars and then inverse the selection.

49. In the Channels Palette, while pressing and **HOLDING** the Command Key (Mac) OR Control Key (PC), click on the Jar 1 Channel to load the channel as a selection.

50. Still **HOLDING** the Command Key (Mac) OR Control Key (PC), HOLD the SHIFT KEY as well to ADD to the selection. Now click on the Jar 2 Channel, the Jar 3 Channel, the Jar 4 Channel and the Jar 5 Channel - holding the Command Key (Mac) OR Control Key (PC) + the

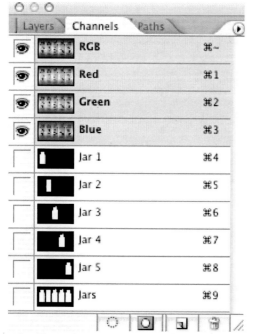

Shift Key. This will select all 5 jars.

51. **SELECT > SAVE SELECTION**.
52. Save the Selection as **JARS**.

53. Now go under the **SELECT** menu again and select **INVERSE**.

54. The background becomes selected.

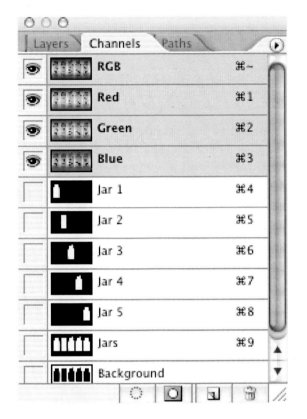

55. **SELECT > SAVE SELECTION**.

56. Save the selection as "Background."

57. **File >Save**.

58. **DESELECT**.

59. **Command + CLICK (Mac) OR Control + CLICK (PC) on the BACKGROUND CHANNEL** - to load the channel as a selection.

60. Click on the **Layers** tab to bring the Layers Palette to the front.

61. **Double-click** on the *Background* Layer and name it "**Jars**."

60. Press the **DELETE KEY**. The background behind the jars disappears and the background is transparent.

62. Open the **Blue Sky.jpg** document.

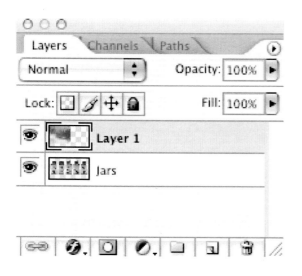

63. Using the **MOVE TOOL**, Overlap the Blue Sky. jpg document over the Floating Jars.psd document so that you can see both documents at once.

64. Make sure the Blue Sky document is activated and click and hold the Blue Sky photo and drag and drop into the Floating Jars document.

65. In the Layers Palette, you will now see 2 layers.

66. Double click on the name **LAYER 1** in the Layers palette and name the layer **Blue Sky**.

67. Drag the Blue Sky layer beneath the Jars layer.

68. You may close the original Blue Sky document.

69. Using the **MOVE TOOL**, drag the Blue Sky and line it up in the top left corner.

70. **EDIT > TRANSFORM > SCALE**.

71. Holding the **Shift Key**, proportionately scale the Blue Sky layer larger until it fills the area behind the jars.

72. Press the **Return/ Enter Key** to make the transformation take effect.

73. **File > Save**.

Blending Modes

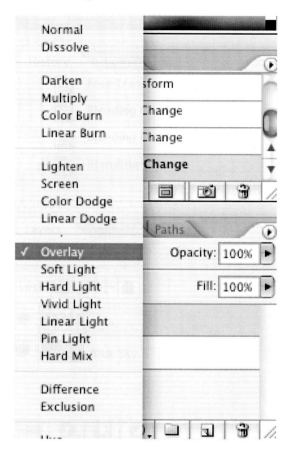

A Blending Mode allows you to combine pixels of one layer with the layers beneath. The particular blending mode you choose will affect the way the layer appears. The layer affected will have a transparent appearance so that you can see the layer beneath without using layer opacity.

74. Click on the Jars Layer to activate it.

75. With the **JARS** layer activated, click on the drop-down menu on the Layers Palette that says "**NORMAL**."

76. Select the "**OVERLAY** " blending mode. The jars become semi-transparent so that the Blue Sky shows through.

Floating Jars.psd @ 15% (Jars, RGB/8)

15%   Doc: 31.5M/116.3M

77. Experiment with other Blending Modes.

78. **File > Save**.

You may close the document.

You have finished this Workshop Tutorial.

Remember to drag your desktop folder to your USB Flash Drive or burn to a CD.

Workshop 3 – Pen Tool and Paths

OBJECTIVE: After completing this Workshop Tutorial, you will be able to use the pen Tool in Adobe Photoshop® to create paths which will allow you to make complicated selections. You will learn how to modify the paths, convert the paths into selections and create clipping paths to use in other applications..

Create a folder on your desktop and name it "Photoshop Tutorial 3." Save all files during the Workshop to this folder. At the end of this tutorial, drag your desktop folder to your USB Flash Drive or burn on a CD.

DRAG TO YOUR DESKTOP FOLDER FROM YOUR CD: Photoshop Tutorial 3 Images

The Pen Tool

1. Open Adobe Photoshop.®

The Pen Tool allows you to have more control over your selections in Adobe Photoshop®. With the Pen Tool you are able to create precise lines and shapes that have a combination of straight and curved lines. The Pen Tool creates vector paths. Paths are made up of anchor points. In order to create a straight line with the Pen Tool, simply click the mouse to create an anchor point and click the mouse in another area on your page to finish the line. In order to create a curved path, you must click and hold the mouse button using the Pen Tool, and drag to create a direction line. You will then click and drag to finish the curved line.

2. Open Pen Tool Exercise 1.jpg.

3. In your Toolbox, select the **PEN TOOL** 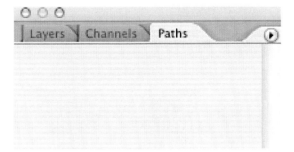 .

4. In the **OPTIONS BAR**, make sure that "**PATHS**" is selected (the 2nd option from the left - instead of SHAPE LAYERS) and the **AUTO/DELETE** option is checked.

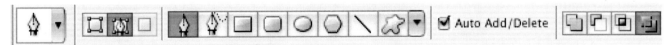

5. Click on the **Paths Palette** tab to bring the palette to the front of its group. The Paths Palette displays thumbnail previews of the paths you draw.

6. Command (Mac) + 0 (zero) OR Control (PC) + 0 (zero) to **Fit on Screen**.

Drawing Straight Paths

Straight Paths are created by clicking the mouse button. The first time you click, you set a starting point for a path. Each time you click afterwards, a straight line is drawn between the previous point and the current point.

7. Using the **PEN TOOL, click on point #1 and let go of your mouse button**.

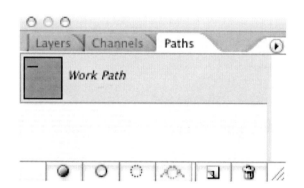

8. **Click on point #2 and let go of the mouse button**. You have created a straight line. If you hold the Shift Key while you use the Pen Tool, it will constrain you to a perfectly straight line.

9. As you draw Paths a temporary storage area named "**Work Path**" appears in the Paths Palette to keep track of the paths you draw.

10. Before starting a new path, you need to end your straight path by either **clicking on the PEN TOOL** in the Toolbox to complete your path or holding the Command Key (Mac) or Control Key (PC) and clicking the mouse on a blank area of the document to deselect the path. Otherwise, the next path you draw will be connected to the first path.

11. The points that connect the Paths are called **ANCHOR POINTS**. You can drag individual anchor points to edit segments of a path with the **DIRECT SELECTION TOOL** (the white arrow) , or you can select all the anchor points to select the entire path with **PATH SELECTION TOOL** (the black arrow) .

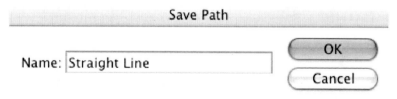

12. In the Paths Palette, double-click the **Work Path** to open the **SAVE PATH** dialog box. Enter "**STRAIGHT LINE**" in the name text box and click **OK** to rename the path.

You must save a *Work Path* to avoid losing its contents. If you deselect the *Work Path* without saving the path and then begin drawing with the Pen Tool again, a new *Work Path* will replace the first one.

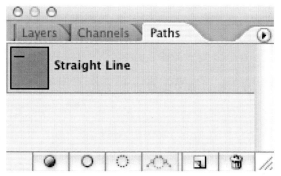

13. In the **Paths Palette**, you will see the *Work Path* has been renamed **Straight Line**. This path will be saved with the file.

14. **File > Save As > Pen Tool 1.psd. Make sure you choose under FORMATS > Photoshop.**

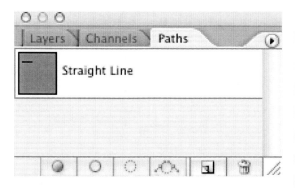

15. In the Paths Palette, click in the **BLANK AREA below the "Straight Line" path to TURN OFF the path before continuing.** If you do not turn off the path before continuing on to a new path, the new path will be added to the Straight Line path. When the path is turned off, the path is hiding in the document and you no longer see the path in your document (as if there was an eye icon to turn the path off like the Layers Palette).

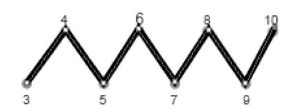

16. Using the **PEN TOOL**, you will click on each point in the zig zag, starting with #3.

17. When you finish clicking the **PEN TOOL** on point #10, **click on the PEN TOOL in the Toolbox to end the path**.

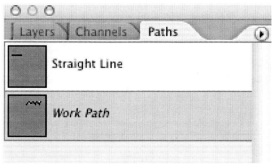

18. In the Paths Palette, double-click on the new *Work Path* and **save the path as "Zig Zag."**

Creating Closed Paths

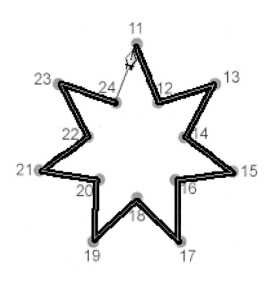

19. Next, you will **trace the star shape**. Starting on point #11, click on each of the numbered points until you get to point #24.

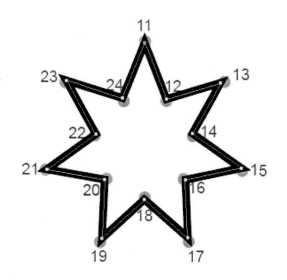

20. You need to continue to click the mouse using the **PEN TOOL** to close the path at #11. When you click back on #11 to close the path, you will see a circle at the top of the **PEN TOOL** indicating that you will be closing a path.

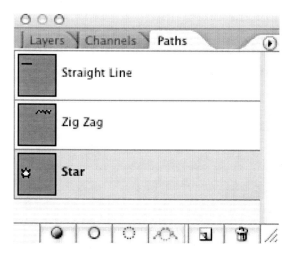

21. Double-click the new Work Path in the Paths Palette and name the path "**Star**."

22. **File > Save**.

23. Before you give the star shape a fill or a stroke, you need to create a new layer.

24. Click on the Layers Palette tab to bring the Layers Palette to the front of the group.

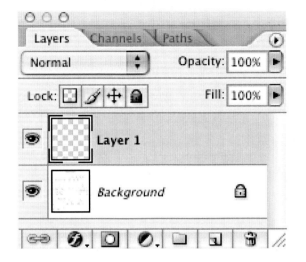

25. Click on the "New Layer" icon at the bottom of the Layers Palette (if you "mouse over" the icons at the bottom of the palette, you will see the names of the icons pop up).

You want to make sure that you paint your vector lines and shapes on a new layer or separate layers. Once filled or outlined, the shapes become objects that will move with the MOVE TOOL or can be edited with selection tools instead of the PEN TOOL, PATH SELECTION or DIRECT SELECTION TOOL.

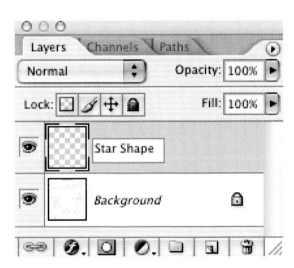

26. Double-click on the WORD "Layer 1" and rename the layer "**Star Shape**." Make sure you are actively on the Star Shape layer before giving the star a fill or a stroke.

27. Click on the Paths Palette to bring the palette to the front of the group.

Giving the Paths a Fill or a Stroke

If you are using paths to draw vector shapes for illustration, the paths will not print unless given a fill or a stroke. Filling a path adds pixels that appear when you print the image. When you fill a path, you can fill it with a color, image or a pattern. Stroking a path will outline the path in color. To fill or stroke a path, you must first select the path with the **PATH SELECTION TOOL** or the **DIRECT SELECTION TOOL** .

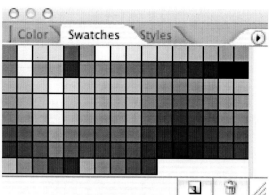

28. Click the **SWATCHES** Palette tab to bring the palette forward. You must **FIRST choose a color** before you can paint the path.

29. **Choose a color swatch** in the Swatches Palette to select a Foreground Color to use to give the star a stroke outline.

30. You must select a painting tool and set the options or attributes (such as the size of the brush or pencil) **BEFORE** you select the tool in the **STROKE DIALOG BOX**.

31. **Click and hold on the BRUSH TOOL to get the PENCIL TOOL**.

32. In the **OPTIONS BAR, choose a #5 diameter brush with 100% hardness**.

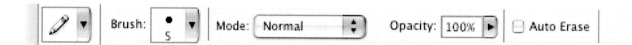

33. Select the **PATH SELECTION TOOL** .

34. Select the Star Path in the Paths Palette.

35. In the Paths Palette, there is a **FLYOUT MENU** on the top right side of the palette. It is accessed by pressing and holding on the small arrow in the circle.

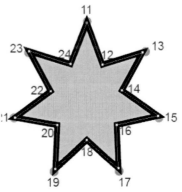

36. When you **click and hold on the FLYOUT ARROW**, you have options for your palette.

37. Click the **FLYOUT ARROW** and choose "**Stroke Path**."

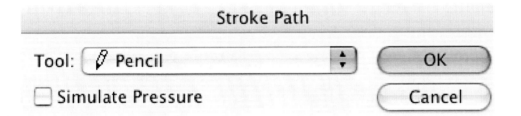

38. Click OK. The path is outlined with the current PENCIL TOOL settings.

39. Choose a different color in the Swatches Palette.

40. **Click and hold on the FLYOUT ARROW of the Paths Palette and select "Fill Path."**

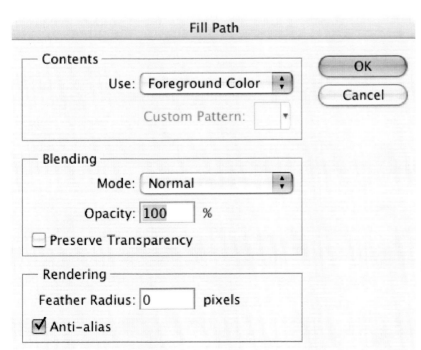

41. When the Fill Path options dialog box appears, make sure **USE: is set to Foreground Color**.

42. Click OK.

43. File > Save.

44. Click on the Layers Palette tab to bring it to the front of the group.

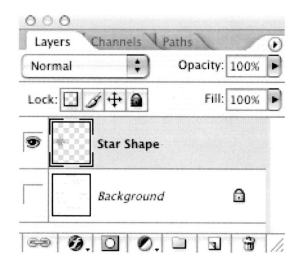

45. Select the **MOVE TOOL** .

46. Click on the **EYE ICON** on the Background Layer to hide the layer.

47. Click on the Star Shape Layer to activate it.

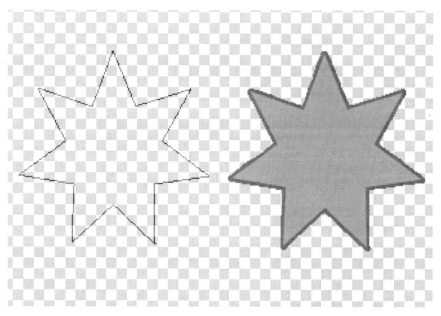

48. Using the **MOVE TOOL**, move the star.

49. The star moves independently of the Star Path.

50. Drag the Star Shape layer into the Trash Can icon on the bottom right side of the Layers Palette.

50. Click on the Path Palette tab to bring the Paths Palette to the front of the group.

Curved Lines

The next set of Pen Tool exercises involve curved lines. To create the curved lines, you will be clicking the mouse and holding the click to drag to another area to create the direction line.

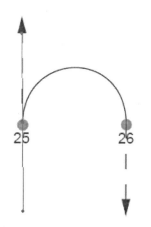

Make sure you turn off the Star path in the Paths Palette by clicking in a blank area below the path names in the palette.

51. Using the **PEN TOOL**, click and **HOLD** on the point at #25 and **DRAG upwards towards the top arrowhead. Make sure you stop in a blank area beneath the arrowhead so that you can see the directional line point. When you let go of the mouse button, you see a gray directional line (Handles).**

52. In order to complete the curve, click and **HOLD on #26** and **DRAG downwards** to that arrow point. Let go of the mouse button.

53.. The curve has extended past the guidelines. Select the **DIRECT SELECTION TOOL**, the white arrow - which is **beneath** the **PATH SELECTION TOOL** and click on the left anchor point (at point #25) to select the point. Now click the directional line anchor point located at the top of the line. Click and hold that point to control the curve.

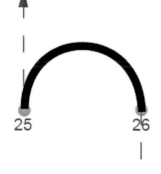

54. Once you have adjusted the directional lines, the curve fits the template.

55. In the Paths Palette, double-click on the *Work Path* and **save the path as Curve 1**.

56. **File > Save**.

57. Click in a blank area in the Paths Palette to deselect the Path.

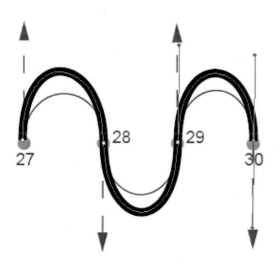

58. You will make a continuous curve. Select the **Pen Tool**. Click and **HOLD on #27** and DRAG upwards to the arrow point. Let go of the mouse button.

59. Click and **HOLD on #28** and **DRAG downwards** to the arrow point.

60. Click and **HOLD on #29 and DRAG upwards** to the arrow point.

61. Click and **HOLD on #30** and **DRAG downwards** to the arrow point.

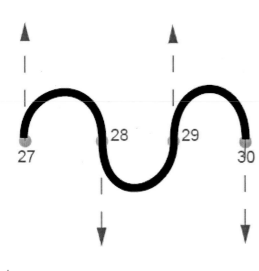

62.. Using the **Direct Selection Tool** (the white arrow) adjust the directional lines so that your curve fits the template.

63. In the Paths Palette, double-click on the *Work Path* and **save the path as Curve 2**.

64. Click in a blank area in the Paths Palette to deselect the Path.

65. **File > Save**.

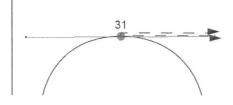

66. You will draw a circle next. **Using the PEN TOOL, click and HOLD on #31** and **DRAG to the right** to the arrow point. Let go of your mouse button.

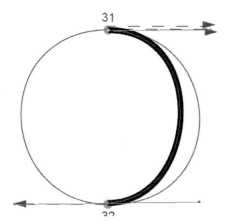

67. **Click and HOLD on #32** and **DRAG to the left** to the arrow point.

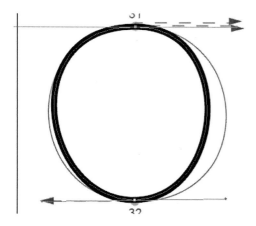

68. **Click and HOLD again on #31** and **DRAG** to the **right** to the arrow point to close the path.

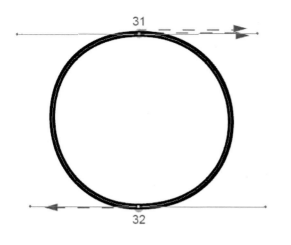

69. Using the **Direct Selection Tool**, drag the directional handles anchor points to make your curve fit the template.

70. In the Paths Palette, double-click on the *Work Path* and **save the path as Circle**.

71. Click in a blank area in the Paths Palette to deselect the Path.

72. File > Save.

73. The next line will combine straight and curved lines. Click on #33 and let go of the mouse button.

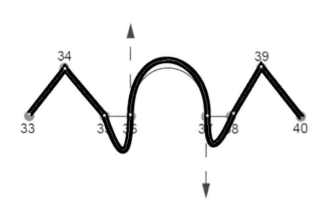

74. Click and #34 and #35.

75. On #36, click and HOLD your mouse button and DRAG upwards to the arrow point.

76. Click and HOLD on #37 and DRAG downwards to the arrow point.

77. Click on #38.

78. Click on #39 and #40.

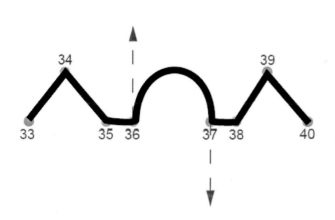

79. Using your **Direct Selection Tool**, click on the directional line anchor point to manipulate each **directional line** to fit the template curve. Your finished curve should look similar to the illustration on the left..

80. In the Paths Palette, double-click on the *Work Path* and **save the path as Curve 3**.

81. **File > Save.**

You may close this document.

Changing the Direction of a Curve

82.. File > Open > Pen Tool Exercise 2.jpg.

83. **File > SAVE AS > Pen Tool 2.psd. Make sure you choose Photoshop as the Format.**

84. Using your **Pen Tool**, click and **HOLD on #1 and DRAG upwards** to the arrow point. Let go of your mouse button.

As you draw the curve, it will look like a continuous curve. We will change the direction of the curve after we draw the curve.

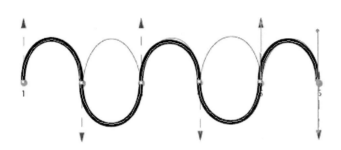

85. Click and **HOLD on #2 and DRAG downwards** to the arrow point. Let go of your mouse button.

86. Click and **HOLD on #3 and DRAG upwards** to the arrow point. Let go of your mouse button.

87. Click and **HOLD on #4 and DRAG downwards** to the arrow point. Let go of your mouse button.

88. Click and **HOLD on #5 and DRAG upwards** to the arrow point. Let go of your mouse button.

89. Click and **HOLD on #6 and DRAG downwards** to the arrow point. Let go of your mouse button.

90. After you finish the curve on #6, select the **Direct Selection Tool**.

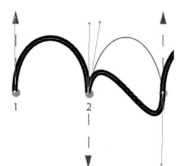

91. Using the **Direct Selection Tool** , you will **select #2 anchor point** (the one on the #2). By doing this, you activate the directional lines for that anchor point.

92. Press and **HOLD the OPTION Key** (the ALT Key for the PC) and **DRAG** the bottom directional line point up to **match the top directional line.** Let go of the mouse button and then the Option Key.

When the **Option Key (the ALT Key for the PC) is pressed** while using the PEN TOOL, the **PEN TOOL becomes the CONVERT POINT TOOL** , which allows you to change the direction of the Path while drawing.

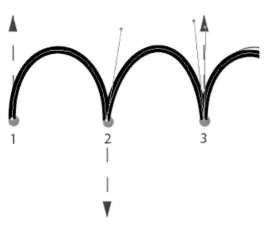

93. Using the **Direct Selection Tool**, you will **select #3 anchor point.**

94. Press and **HOLD the OPTION Key** (the ALT Key for the PC) and **DRAG** the bottom directional line point up to **match the top directional line.** Let go of the mouse button and then the Option Key.

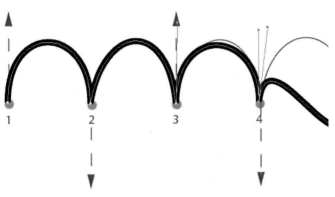

95. Using the **Direct Selection Tool**, you will **select #4 anchor point.**

96. Press and **HOLD the OPTION Key** (the ALT Key for the PC) and **DRAG** the bottom directional line point up to **match the top directional line.** Let go of the mouse button and then the Option Key.

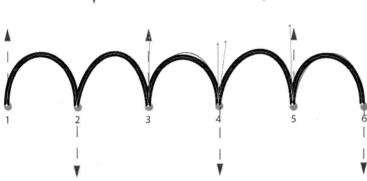

97. Using the **Direct Selection Tool**, you will **select #5 anchor point.**

98. Press and **HOLD the OPTION Key** (the ALT Key for the PC) and **DRAG** the bottom directional line point up to **match the top directional line.** Let go of the mouse button and then the Option Key.

99. In the **Paths Palette**, double-click on the *Work Path* and **save the path as Curve**.

100. Click in a blank area in the Paths Palette to deselect the Path.

101. File > Save.

In order to draw the heart, you must draw a circle first and change the direction of the curve.

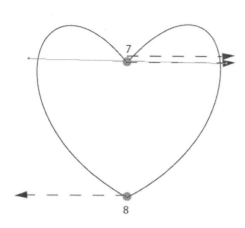

102. Using the PEN TOOL click and **HOLD on the #7 point** and **DRAG to the right arrow point**. Let go of your mouse button.

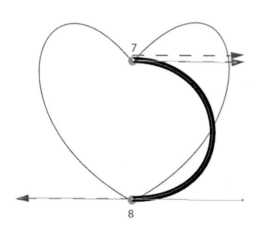

103. Click and **HOLD on #8** and **DRAG to the left arrow point**. Let go of the mouse button.

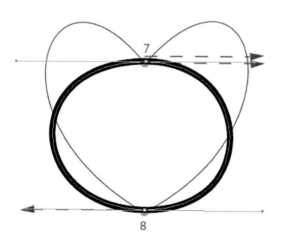

104. Click and **HOLD on #7 again** and **DRAG to the right** to close the path.

105. With the top anchor point already selected, click on the **Direct Selection Tool** .

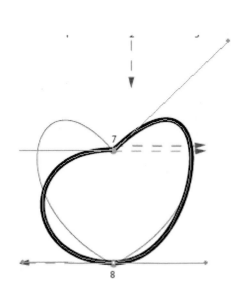

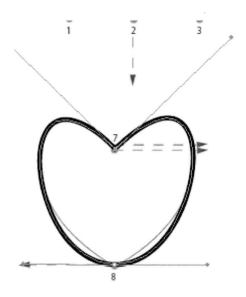

106. Press and **HOLD the OPTION Key** (ALT Key for the PC) and **DRAG the right top directional line point upwards and to the right** as in the illustration. Let go of the mouse button, then the Option Key.

107. **Drag the left top directional line point upwards and to the left**. Adjust the handles as necessary.

108. Click on the bottom anchor point to select it.

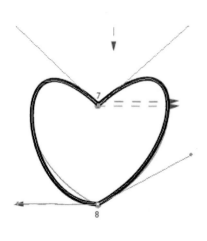

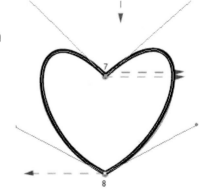

109. Press and **HOLD the OPTION Key** (ALT Key for the PC) and **DRAG the right bottom directional line point upwards and to the right** as in the illustration. Let go of the mouse button, then the Option Key.

110. Drag the **left bottom directional line point upwards and to the left.** Adjust the handles as necessary.

110. Go to the **Layers Palette**.

111. Create a new layer. Name it "**Heart**."

112. Go to the Paths Palette.

113. Choose a color in the **Swatches Palette**.

114. Click and hold on the **Flyout Arrow on the Paths Palette** and select "**Fill Path**."

115. The Heart fills with the color you chose. **Choose another color in the Swatches Palette**.

116. Click and hold on the **Flyout Arrow in the Paths Palette** and select "**Stroke Path**." The Heart is outlined in the color you chose.

117. Go to the Layers Palette and **turn off the Eye Icon** next to the *Background* layer to see only the Heart layer. **Now go back and turn the Eye Icon back *on* next to the *Background* layer.**

118. File > Save.

Adding and Subtracting Anchor Points

You can **add anchor points to paths** using the **ADD ANCHOR POINT TOOL** accessed **under the PEN TOOL**. To add the anchor point, simply have the path selected and using the **ADD ANCHOR POINT TOOL**, click on the path to add an anchor point.

You can **delete anchor points from paths** if you have too many points on the path. The fewer points on the path or curve, the smoother the path or curve will be. The **DELETE ANCHOR POINT TOOL** will delete an anchor point on a path simply by using the tool and clicking on the unwanted anchor point.

Converting Points

To **convert a curve to a straight line or vice versa**, use the **CONVERT POINT TOOL**. Using the CONVERT POINT TOOL is similar to drawing with the PEN TOOL. To convert an anchor point to a corner point, you click the anchor point with the CONVERT POINT TOOL. To convert a corner point to a curve, you need to click an hold on the corner point with the CONVERT POINT TOOL and drag to create the control handles.

119. The **FREEFORM PEN TOOL** creates a path by dragging like the PENCIL TOOL. Be aware that the FREEFORM PEN TOOL creates **MANY** anchor points and that this effect may be undesirable due to excessive editing of anchor points.

Drawing the Apple

120. Create a new layer and name it "Apple." Make sure you are on the Apple layer.

121. Go to the paths Palette and deselect any paths.

122. Using the PEN TOOL, draw the apple in the Pen Tool Exercise 2.

123. **DO NOT click only**. You **MUST click and drag to create curved lines**. Remember that the Option Key (ALT Key for the PC) changes the direction of the curve.

124. Make separate paths out of the apple, leaf and stem.

125. Name the paths.

126. Fill the apple, leaf and stem with appropriate colors.

127. After you've completed the Apple, **File > Save**.

You may close this file after you have completed the Apple.

Clipping Paths

A **CLIPPING PATH** is a way to save an image (such as a logo) with a **transparent background** when placing into a page-layout program. You will draw a Path, save the Path, make it into a **CLIPPING PATH**, and **save the file as an EPS** to place in a page-layout program such as Adobe InDesign®. A **CLIPPING PATH** is a sharp-edged shape (a vector shape) versus a rasterized selection using a selection tool (such as the LASSO TOOL). Thus, you get a cleaner, sharper - plus VECTOR selection. You can also create a Vector Mask in the Layers palette using the PEN TOOL, which acts like a Layer Mask yet it is a vector, sharp edged shape. However, we will be using the CLIPPING PATH option in the Flyout of the Paths Palette in this tutorial.

128. **Open Vase.jpg**.

129. Command + 0 (zero) for the Mac OR Control + 0 (zero) for the PC to Fit on Screen.

130. Click on the **PEN TOOL** in the Toolbox.

131. In the **OPTIONS BAR**, make sure that "**PATHS**" is selected (the 2nd option from the left - instead of SHAPE LAYERS) and the **AUTO/DELETE** option is checked.

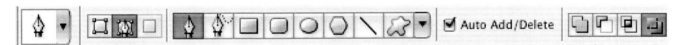

132. Begin to trace the outline of the Vase with the **PEN TOOL**. Remember to **CLICK and DRAG the mouse while tracing to create curved anchor points and lines**.

133. Be patient and draw SLOWLY. Draw in the direction that you are tracing.

134. You will be able to edit your tracing with the **DIRECT SELECTION TOOL** .

135. After tracing the pitcher **SLOWLY**, you can close the path.

136. Use the **DIRECT SELECTION TOOL** and adjust your anchor points and handles to fit the vase.

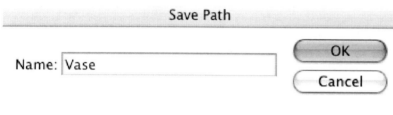

137. Click on the Path Palette. Double-click on the *Work Path* and **save the path as "Vase."**

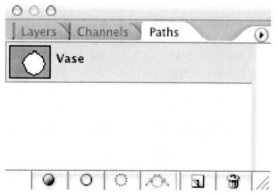

138. In the Paths Palette, the *Work Path* changes to a saved path.

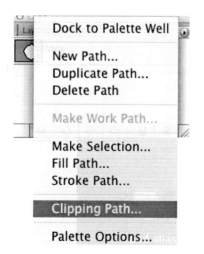

139. Once the path is saved, you are ready to create a CLIPPING PATH. **Click on the FLYOUT of the Paths Palette and select CLIPPING PATH.**

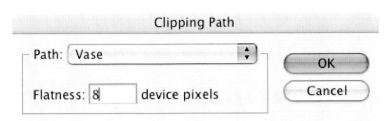

140. When the Clipping Path dialog box appears, **type 8 in the Flatness area.** A flatness setting from 8 - 10 is recommended for high-resolution printing (1200 dpi - 2400 dpi); a setting from 1 to 3 for low-resolution printing (300 dpi to 600 dpi).

141. Click OK.

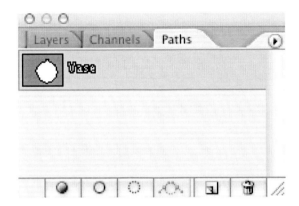

142. In the Paths Palette the word Vase is outlined if you have a Mac to show you have created a CLIPPING PATH. If you are working on a PC, you will not see any difference.

143. With the CLIPPING PATH still turned on, **FILE > SAVE AS > Vase.eps (a Photoshop EPS).**

144. When you place the photograph into a page-layout program, only the vase will be imported and not the background behind the vase (or a white background behind the vase). **IT MUST BE SAVED AS AN .EPS FILE FORMAT.**

Clipping Path saved as a Photoshop EPS.

No Clipping Path . Background image is showing.

The vase was selected - the selection was Inversed (the background then became selected - then Deleted) and the image was saved with a "transparent" background. However, once the image is saved, the background becomes white if a Clipping Path is not made.

Creating a Selection from a Path

145. You can make a selection from the path by loading the path as a selection (just as you have loaded Alpha Channels as selections previously).

146. In the **Paths Palette**, hold down the **Command Key** (Mac) OR Control Key (PC) and **click on the VASE path to load the path as a selection.**

147. If you would like to soften the edge a little to place the vase into another photograph, you need to feather the selection.

148. **SELECT > FEATHER.**

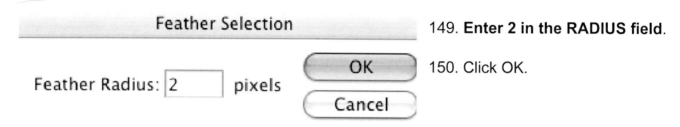

149. **Enter 2 in the RADIUS field.**

150. Click OK.

151. EDIT > COPY.

152. Open Fruit Vase.jpg.

153. Fit on Screen.

154. EDIT > PASTE.

155. The Vase is now in the Fruit Vase photo.

156. FILE > SAVE AS > FRUIT VASE COMPOSITE.psd.

157. You need to create a shadow the same way you did for the clowns in Tutorial 1.

158. Rename Layer 1 to Vase.

159. Command + J (or Control + J for the PC) to copy and paste the Vase layer.

160. Drag the new Vase Copy layer **below** the Vase layer in the Layers Palette.

161. Double-click on the **WORD** Vase Copy to rename the Layer to **Vase Shadow**.

162. **Edit > Transform > DISTORT**. This will allow you to distort the layer to appear as if the vase has a shadow.

163. Drag the middle handle of the transformation box down and out to the left of the Vase. Try to match the angle of the Fruit Vase's natural shadow.

164. Adjust the transformation so that the base of the shadow and the base of the Vase match as in the image below. **Press the RETURN / ENTER Key** to make the transformation take effect.

165. Hold down the **Command Key (the Control Key for the PC) and click on the LAYER THUMBNAIL** of the Clown 3 Shadow layer in the Layers Palette to load the layer as a selection.

166. Press the **DELETE** Key. The image inside of the selection is now deleted.

Feather Selection

Feather Radius: 20 pixels

OK
Cancel

167. **Select Menu > Feather**.

168. Enter **20 in the Feather Radius** box in the dialog box that appears. **Click OK**.

169. **Select > Inverse**.

170. Press the **Delete Key**.

171. **File > Save**.

172, Click on the Foreground Color Swatch in the Toolbox.

173. The Color Picker opens.

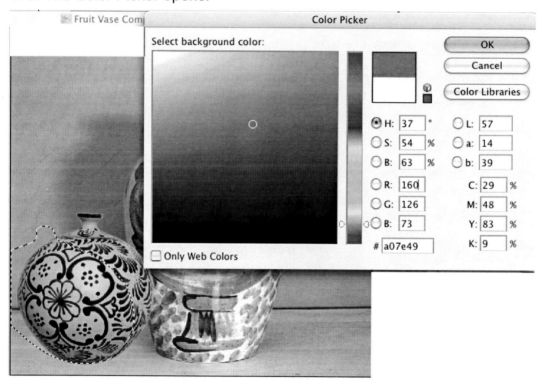

174. Take the cursor outside of the Color Picker Box and you will see an Eyedropper Tool Icon .

175. Sample the shadow behind the Fruit Vase to get a brownish color.

176. Click OK and the Foreground Color changes.

177. Click on the Background Color Swatch in the Toolbox.

178. Take the cursor outside of the Color Picker Box and you will see an Eyedropper Tool Icon .

175. Sample the shadow at the BASE of the Fruit Vase to get a light brown color.

176. Select the **Gradient Tool**  in the Toolbox.

177. In the **Options Bar, make sure the OPACITY % is still 40%.**

178. Using the **Gradient Tool**, press and hold your mouse and drag a gradient from the top of the Vase Shadow to the base of the Vase.

175. **Deselect**.

Your finished shadow should look similar to the image below.

176. File > Close.

You have completed this tutorial.

Remember to drag your desktop folder to your USB Flash Drive after you've completed this tutorial OR BURN TO A CD.

Workshop 4 – Colorizing and Adjusting Color

OBJECTIVE: After completing this Workshop Tutorial, you will be able to convert images into black & white images and add color to those images using several techniques in Adobe Photoshop® . You will learn how to use adjustment layers to color correct images as well as change existing color.

Create a folder on your desktop and name it "Photoshop Tutorial 4." Save all of your files during the Workshop to this folder. At the end of this tutorial, drag your desktop folder to your USB Flash Drive or burn on a CD.

DRAG TO YOUR DESKTOP FOLDER FROM YOUR CD: Photoshop Tutorial 4 Images
In Adobe Photoshop® there are two type of Channels: Alpha Channels (which we have already covered in our first two tutorials) and Color Channels. Color channels give the color information about the image. The most common color modes we use are RGB: Red, Green, Blue; and CMYK: Cyan, Magenta, Yellow, Black. RGB color is projected color, such as your computer monitor. When images are scanned onto a CD, they are in RGB color. CMYK color is for commercial printing. CMYK color channels color separate for printing on a printing press. It is always best to work in the RGB color mode in Photoshop because you will have more options available to you in the program. Only convert to CMYK before going to a commercial press.

Converting images to a grayscale tone - When converting an image from a color mode to a grayscale tone image, you can accomplish this effect in several different ways: Desaturate, Lab Color or through the Channel Mixer.

DESATURATE - The first way is through the **DESATURATE** command. This is an adjustment which is accomplished by going under **IMAGE > ADJUSTMENTS > DESATURATE**. The Desaturate command converts a color image to a grayscale image in the same color mode. For example, it assigns equal red, green, and blue values to each pixel in an RGB image to make it appear grayscale. The lightness value of each pixel does not change.

LAB COLOR - Lab color is the intermediate color model Photoshop uses when converting from one color mode to another. When converting from RGB or CMYK to Grayscale, you should go through Lab Color first, in order to retain luminance, because Lab color has a lightness channel. This Lightness channel retains tonal information when converting color modes. Converting to Lab Color is accomplished by going under **IMAGE > MODE > LAB COLOR**. If you choose to go through Lab Color to convert to Grayscale (IMAGE > MODE > GRAYSCALE), you will need to convert back to RGB (**IMAGE > MODE > RGB**) in order to get a color palette (versus a grayscale palette) to colorize the B & W image.

CHANNEL MIXER - This option of creating a B & W image gives you a wider spread of flexibility to edit in Photoshop to simulate effects of shooting in black and white.

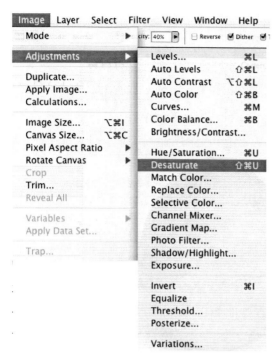

1. Open Adobe Photoshop®.

2. Open **Green Apples.jpg**.

Desaturate

3. You will use the Desaturate command. **IMAGE > ADJUSTMENTS > DESATURATE**.

4. The green is a little dark when it is desaturated into a grayscale.

5. Use the **CURVES** command to lighten the apples. The curves adjustment command is a color and tonal adjustment. It will lighten or darken an image.

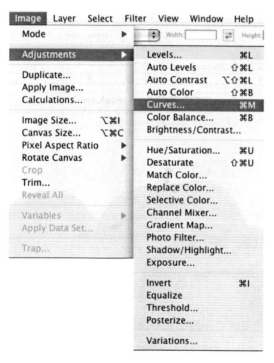

6. **IMAGE > ADJUSTMENTS > CURVES**.

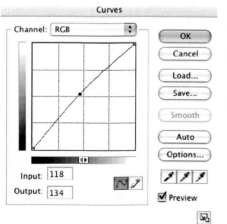

7. In the dialog box, click an hold the diagonal line and pull upwards and to the left JUST SLIGHTLY until the **Input** says 118 and the **Output** says 134. You may have to adjust those numbers slightly. This will lighten the image.

8. The results show the apples have become lighter in tonal values.

9. **FILE > REVERT**. You have reverted the image to the original apples.

Through Lab Color

10. Go under the **IMAGE** menu and select **MODE > Lab Colo**r.

11. Go back under the **IMAGE menu > MODE > GRAYSCALE**.

12. When it prompts you to discard color information, **click OK**. This B & W version does not need to be adjusted.

13. **IMAGE > MODE > RGB**.

14. Now you have a Black & White (grayscale) image but it is actually in the RGB mode. This will allow you to use color to paint the black and white image.

15. Now you will REVERT the photo back to the original version.

16. **FILE > REVERT**.

17. The apples are back to green apples.

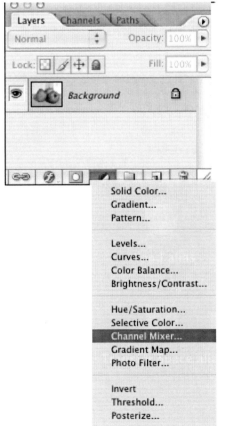

18. Make sure the Layers palette is visible. **Click and hold on the "Create new fill or adjustment layer" icon at the bottom of the Layers palette** 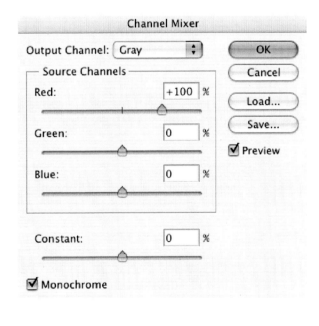 **and choose "Channel Mixer.".**

19. In the **Channel Mixer dialog box**, click the "**Monochrome**" box at the bottom left side of the dialog box. The image becomes a black and white image.

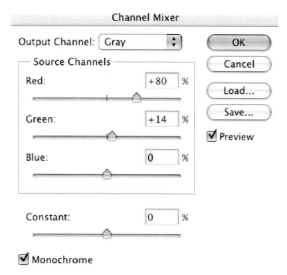

20. **Slide the Red down to +80**.

21. Slide the **Green up to +14** and click the **OK** button.

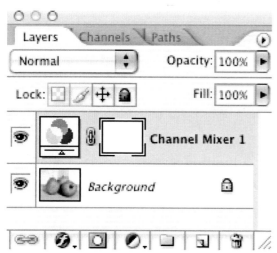

22. You can see the Channel Mixer Adjustment Layer in the Layers palette. **Adjustment Layers** affect only the layers beneath the Adjustment Layer.

23. **FILE > SAVE AS > Painted Apples.psd. Make sure you are saving it as a PHOTOSHOP document.**

Selecting the Apples

24. In the Layers palette, create a **New Layer** by either clicking on the **Layers palette flyout > New Layer** or by clicking on the New Layer icon at the bottom of the Layers palette.

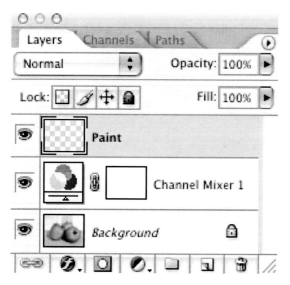

25. Name the new layer **PAINT**.

26. You will paint on this layer **ONLY** to preserve the original image. If you do not like the results of your painting, you can either discard the Paint layer and create a new one or use the Eraser tool to erase the areas of paint that you dislike.

27. Now you will begin making individual selections of the three apples.

28. Select the **PEN TOOL** from the Toolbox. **Remember to choose "PATHS" in the Options Bar before drawing.**

29. Using the **PEN TOOL, select the apple on the left. REMEMBER TO CLICK AND DRAG THE PEN TOOL** to create a curved path.

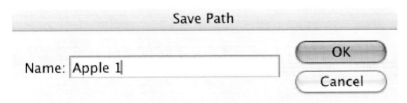

30. Go to the **Paths Palette** and double-click on the *Work Path* and name it "**Apple 1**" to save the Path.

31. Using the **Direct Selection Tool** (under the Path Selection Tool) manipulate and adjust the anchor points to fit the apple.

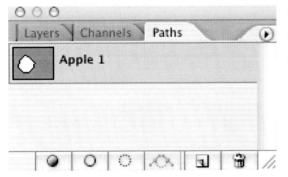

32. **Hold down the Command Key** (Mac) or the Control Key (PC) and **click on the name "Apple 1"** in the Paths Palette **to load the path as a selection**.

33. Save the selection (**SELECT > SAVE SELECTION**) as **APPLE 1**. Click OK.

34. **Command + D** (Mac) or **Control + D** (PC) to **DESELECT**.

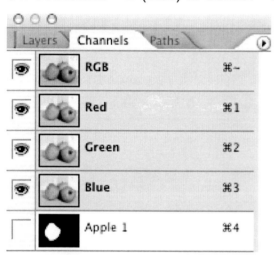

If you click on the **Channels Palette**, you can see the Apple 1, Alpha Channel (your saved selection).

35. **FILE > SAVE**.

36. Using the **PEN TOOL, select the center apple**.

37. When you have completed the Path, in the **Paths Palette**, double-click on the *Work Path* and save the path as "**Apple 2**."

38. **Hold down the Command Key** (Mac) or the Control Key (PC) and **click on the name "Apple 2"** in the Paths Palette **to load the path as a selection**.

39. **SELECT > SAVE SELECTION**.

40. Name the **Alpha Channel** (saved selection) **Apple 2**.

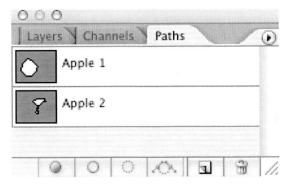

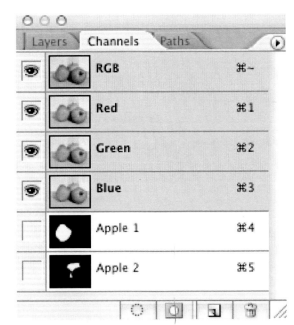

41. **DESELECT**.

42. You now should have **2 Paths and 2 Alpha Channels**.

43. **FILE > SAVE**.

44. Using the **PEN TOOL, select the apple on the right** .

45. After you have completed the Path, in the **Paths Palette**, double-click on the *Work Path* and save the path as "**Apple 3**."

46. **Hold down the Command Key** (Mac) or the Control Key (PC) and **click on the name "Apple 3"** in the Paths Palette **to load the path as a selection**.

47. **SELECT > SAVE SELECTION**.

48. Name the **Alpha Channel** (saved selection) **Apple 3**.

49. **FILE > SAVE**.

Painting

50. Now you are ready to Paint. Make sure you are on the Paint Layer.

51. Click on the Channels tab and pull the Channels tab away from the Layers palette to make the Channels palette separate. This way you can see both the Layers palette and the Channels palette at the same time (to avoid painting on the original, background layer).

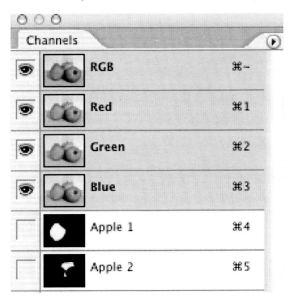

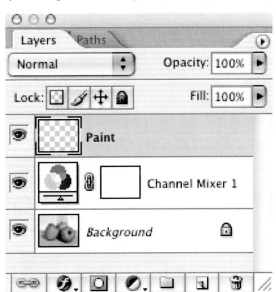

52. You will need to load the Apple 1 channel as a selection.

53. **There are three ways to load a channel as a selection**.

　　　1). Go under the Select menu > Load selection.

　　　2). In the Channels palette, drag the Alpha Channel down to the "Load Channel as a Selection"  icon on the bottom of the Layers palette (the left icon on the bottom of the Channels palette).

　　　3). Hold down the **Command Key** (Control Key for the PC) and click on the Alpha Channel in the Channels palette.

54. After you have loaded the Apple 1 channel as a selection, you will **choose a color** in either the Swatches Palette or the Foreground Swatch in the Toolbox.

55. Select the **BRUSH TOOL**.

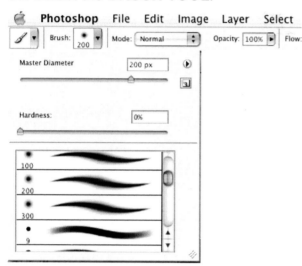

57. In the **OPTIONS BAR**, choose a **#200 Soft Brush**.

58. Next, in then **OPTIONS BAR**, change the **OPACITY to 20%**.

59. Paint the selection with a color. You may add other colors within that apple to give the apple an airbrushed look.

60. **DESELECT** after you have finished painting the apple.

61. **Load the Apple 2 Alpha Channel as a selection** .

62. Choose a color and paint Apple 2 with the 20% opacity paint brush. Again, remember to paint only on the "Paint" layer, not the background layer.

63. **FILE >SAVE**.

64. **DESELECT**.

65. **Load the Apple 3 Alpha Channel** as a selection.

66. Choose a color and **paint Apple 3** with the 20% opacity BRUSH TOOL.

67. **FILE > SAVE**.

69. **DESELECT**.

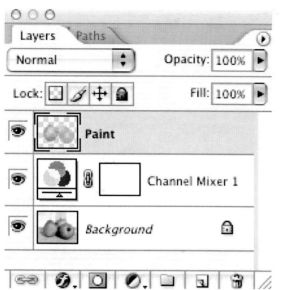

70. You may use the **ERASER TOOL**  to erase the stems out of the color tint of the apples.

Save your document.

Using the Hue and Saturation Adjustment

70. Now you have finished the Paint project. You will next "Paint" the black & white apple image using only the color adjustment Hue and Saturation instead of using the Brush Tool. The Hue command will change the color of the apples and the Saturation command will change the intensity of the color.

71. **After saving the Paint document for the final time, take the Paint Layer and drag it into the trash can on the Layers palette.**

72. **FILE > SAVE AS > HUESATURATION.PSD**

73. You need to **FLATTEN** the document to use this command.

74. Click and hold the **FLYOUT ARROW of the Layers Palette** (on the top right of the palette) and choose "**Flatten Image.**"

75. You will be using the Hue/Saturation color adjustment on the *Background Layer* in this document.

76. **Load the Apple 1 Alpha Channel** as a selection.

77. Go under **IMAGE > ADJUSTMENTS > HUE/SATURATION**.

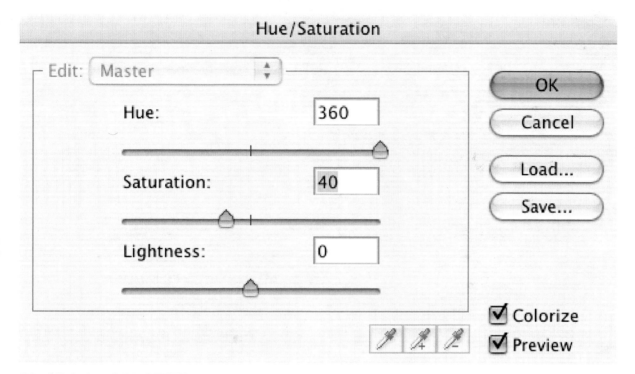

78. Click the **COLORIZE** box.

79. Slide the **Hue slider to a Red** color.

80. Slide the **Saturation to more saturated (+40)**.

81. Click **OK**.

82. **DESELECT**.

83. **FILE > SAVE**.

84. **Load the Apple 2 Alpha Channel** as a selection.

85. Go under **IMAGE > ADJUSTMENTS > HUE/SATURATION**.

86. Click the **COLORIZE** box.

87. Slide the Hue and Saturation sliders to **make a yellow apple**.

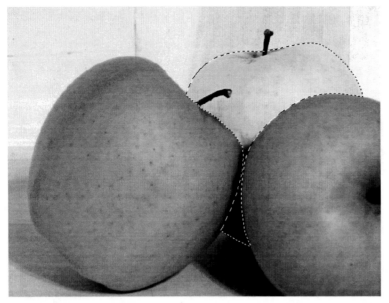

88. **DESELECT**.

89. **FILE > SAVE**.

90. **Load the Apple 3 Alpha Channel** as a selection.

91. Go under **IMAGE > ADJUSTMENTS > HUE/ SATURATION**.

92. Click the **COLORIZE** box.

93. Slide the **Hue and Saturation** sliders to make a **green apple**.

94. **DESELECT**.

95. **FILE > SAVE**.

Applying the Tutorial

96. **Open Oranges.jpg from your folder.**

97. Follow the steps above in this Tutorial and apply the same steps above to the Oranges image.

98. You will make two separate files: **Painted Oranges and HueSaturated Oranges - both PSD (Photoshop) documents**.

99. **FILE > SAVE** when you have finished.

100. **FILE > CLOSE** to close the document.

Changing Existing Color Using Hue and Saturation

101. Open > Star.jpg.

102. Using the PEN TOOL (making sure your PATHS OPTION is still selected), select the star. **REMEMBER TO CLICK AND DRAG THE PEN TOOL** to create a curved path.

103. Using the **Direct Selection Tool** 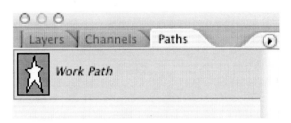 (under the Path Selection Tool) manipulate and adjust the anchor points to fit the star.

104. Go to the **Paths Palette** and double-click on the *Work Path* and name it **"Star"** to save the Path.

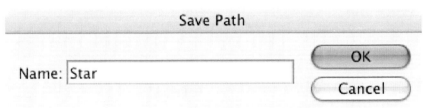

105. In the Paths Palette, **LOAD THE STAR AS A SELECTION by dragging the path into the "Load Path as a selection" icon** at the bottom of the Paths Palette.

106. **SELECT > INVERSE**.

You will use **Hue /Saturation as an Adjustment Layer** this time. Adjustment Layers give you the flexibility to change your mind. The Adjustment Layers affect only the layers beneath but you can trash the Adjustment Layer if you do not like the effect. You can choose the "COLORIZE" box or you can just slide the hue to change the color.

107. Click on the **LAYERS Palette**.

108. Click and hold on the **"Create new fill or adjustment layer" icon** at the bottom of the Layers Palette and select **HUE/SATURATION**.

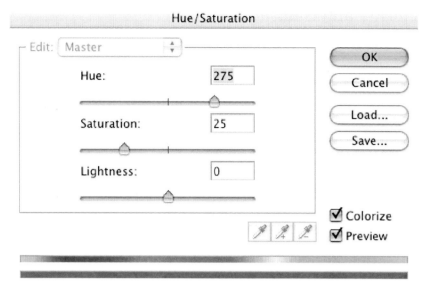

109. Slide the **HUE** slider to change the color of the background.

110. Click the **COLORIZE** box and slide the slider around to see the difference.

111. Click **OK** when you have chosen your color.

112. **DESELECT**.

113. File > Save As > Star.PSD.

You may close the document.

You have finished this Workshop Tutorial.

Remember to drag your desktop folder to your USB Flash Drive or burn on a CD.

Workshop 5 – Retouching and Adjustments

OBJECTIVE: When retouching photographs, one of the most important items to remember is to ensure the image is the correct resolution for the output you are using. For high resolution output, you need to make sure the image is scanned in (or shot on a digital camera) at 300 ppi. Once digitized, an image loses sharpness. The **Unsharp Mask** command actually sharpens digital images. The amount is determined by the photo itself, and every photo is different.

When working with digital images, scanned images or old photographs, tonal and color adjustments may be needed to enhance the tones and colors of photographs. Sometimes these adjustments are needed due to the type of camera, the lighting when the photograph was shot, or the age of the photograph. Other times, you may need to repair damaged photographs. After completing this Workshop Tutorial, you will be able to use **Adjustments Layers** (such as Levels, Curves and Color Balance) to alter the color and tonality of photographs and make repairs to damaged photographs using the Cloning Tool, Spot Healing Brush, Healing Brush and Patch Tool.

Create a folder on your desktop and name it "Photoshop Tutorial 5." Save all files during the Workshop to this folder. At the end of this tutorial, drag your desktop folder to your USB Flash Drive or burn to a CD.

DRAG TO YOUR DESKTOP FOLDER: "Photoshop Tutorial 5 Images" folder

Color Management

Color management is essential in Photoshop to make sure your images output the way you expect them to. While working in RGB, you have the advantage of all of the Photoshop tools, effects and filters - while working in the CMYK mode, you don't. When going to commercial print you must convert the image into a CMYK color mode prior to output. Producing a color profile for your image is an essential part of making sure your image outputs as you expect. This color profile is actually embedded in the file when you save to be read when the image is opened.

Adobe RGB (1998) - This RGB editing space has become the standard for all images that will eventually get converted to the CMYK color mode to go to commercial printers.

Ideally, you should use a calibration system to calibrate and profile your monitor. However, you will at the minimum need to set your color management interface correctly in Photoshop before you begin working with your images.

1. Open Adobe Photoshop.®

2. **EDIT > COLOR SETTINGS**.

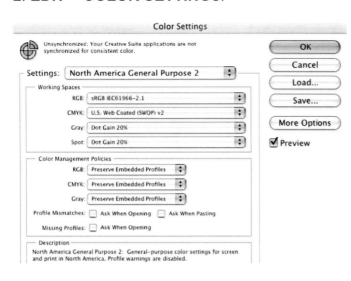

3. The Color Settings Dialog Box appears. Click on the "More Options" button.

4. Click on the drop-down arrow next to "SETTING."

5. Choose "U.S.Prepress Defaults."

6. In the **WORKING SPACES** area, click on the RGB drop-down arrow and choose **ADOBE RGB (1998).**

7. Make sure all of the Color Management boxes are checked alerting you to profile mismatches and missing profiles when opening up images.

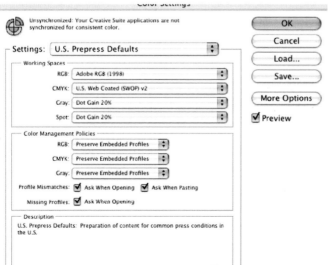

8. Your **COLOR SETTINGS** should match the ones in the box on the left. Click **OK**.

9. File > Browse > Photoshop Tutorial 5 (to open Adobe Bridge®)

10. Navigate to open the photo "Coliseum.tif."

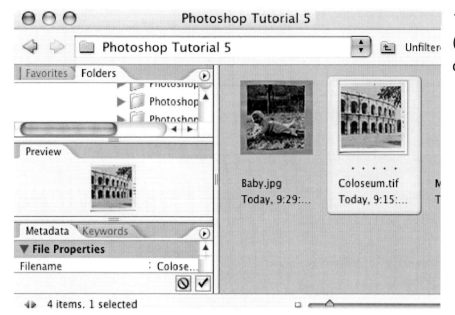

11. **Command + 0** (zero) (Control + 0 for the PC) to Fit on Screen.

12. Using the **Crop Tool**, draw a rectangle around the photograph to crop out the enough so that none of the paper of the photo album from which this image was scanned is showing in the crop preview area. You will see flashing dashes ("Dancing Ants"). You may adjust the cropped area by dragging on the handles of the crop preview box. The area that is outside the cropped area is dark.

13. Press the **Return Key** (Enter Key on the PC) to make the crop take effect.

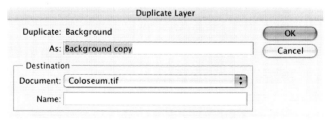

14. Create a **duplicate layer** of the Background by clicking on the **flyout arrow of the Layers palette** and choosing **Duplicate Layer.** Click **OK**.

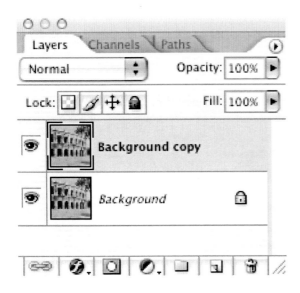

15. By creating a duplicate layer of the photograph, you will preserve the original photograph or scan. The only layer to be affected will be the **Background Copy** layer.

16. File Save As > **Coliseum.PSD** (change the File Format to Photoshop).

17. Make sure you have the **Background Copy layer** activated.

Image Size and Resolution

As mentioned previously, the image size and resolution as it relates to the final output is most important. You should never stretch the pixels.

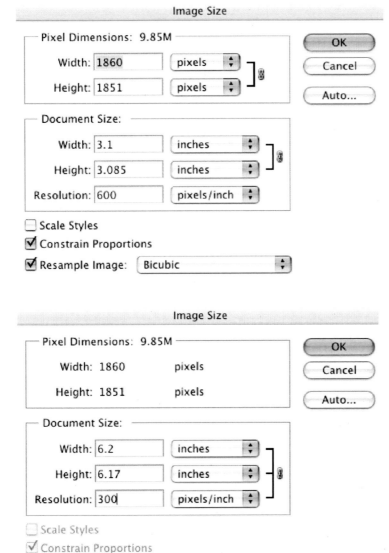

18. Go under **IMAGE > IMAGE SIZE**.

19. The Image Size dialog box appears.

20. This document size is rather small (3.1" X 3.085"). **If you wish to INCREASE the Document Size, you must DECREASE the Resolution proportionately**.

21. The easiest way to change the image size and resolution is to **UNCHECK the RESAMPLE IMAGE** box at the bottom of this dialog box. By unchecking this box, Resolution will decrease proportionately as you increase the width and height in inches.

22. In the **RESOLUTION** field, type in **300**. Notice that the Width and Height in inches doubles, because you divided the resolution by half.

23. Click OK.

24. **FILE > SAVE**.

Applying Unsharp Mask

Ideally, it is best to use the Unsharp Mask filter in phases (two to three phases). Begin with applying the filter on the Background Copy layer. After you color or tonal correct the image, you should sharpen the image again.

25. On the Background Copy layer, go under **FILTER > SHARPEN > UNSHARP MASK**.

There are three Unsharp Mask settings: **Amount, Radius,** and **Threshold**.

> **Amount sets the intensity** of the sharpening effect. The higher the number the sharper the image. Most images require an initial Amount **between 50 and 100%**. Of course this depends on the image. At the output phase, apply a 120 - 200% in the Amount area.

> **Radius** controls the **width of the sharpening** (sometimes referred to as a "halo"). The higher the radius, the sharper the edges of the pixels (which create the "halo"). Initially, you might want to use a 0.5 to 1 for a Radius setting. However, when going to the output phase, you will need to apply an additional 1.0 to 2.0 Radius (especially for inkjet output).

> **Threshold** controls **which pixels** and the amount the pixels are sharpened. This effect helps decide which adjacent pixels are affected according to tonal value. The lower the setting, more pixels are affected. The higher the setting, the more contrast you will see in the image. Start off with a low Threshold (0 - 1) and increase it only if needed.

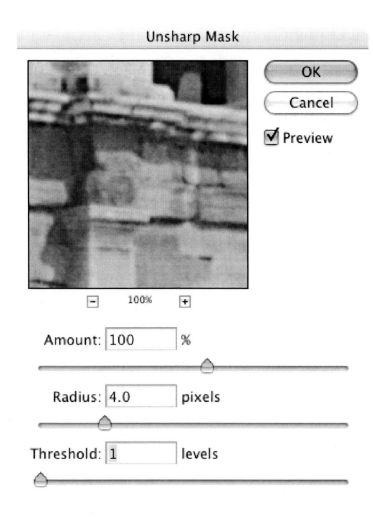

26. The **Unsharp Mask** dialog box opens.

27. Enter **100 in the AMOUNT** field, **4.0 in the RADIUS** field and a **THRESHOLD of 1.**

28. Click OK.

29. FILE > SAVE.

30. Turn the **EYE ICON off** 👁 on the Background Copy layer to see the effects of the sharpening. **Afterwards, turn the Eye Icon back on**.

Adjustment Layers

Adjustment Layers are color and tonal correction layers that affect the layers beneath the Adjustment Layers. The advantage of creating adjustments on Adjustment Layers is that they

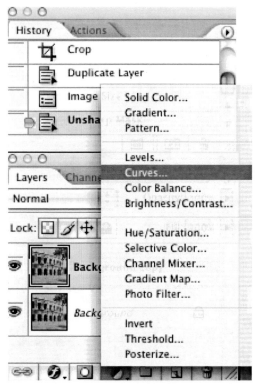

are temporary and can be easily deleted if you are not satisfied with the effects. The adjustment Layers are meant to build upon another. This means once you have color corrected using an Adjustment Layer, you must add the additional Adjustment Layer on top of the original Adjustment Layer.

31. Make sure the **Background Copy layer** is activated.

32. Click and hold on the **"Create new fill or adjustment layer" icon** ⬤. at the bottom of the Layers Palette and select **CURVES**.

The Curves Adjustment corrects color in an image by allowing you to adjust the highlights and shadows, as well as the midtones. You can also select the Channels drop-down menu in the Curves dialog box and edit tones on those Channels.

 33. In the Curves dialog box, select the **EYEDROPPER on the right** (the "Set White Point" eyedropper in the lower right area of the Curves dialog box).

34. Take the EYEDROPPER and **click on a light part of an arch** in the photo on the right side of the Coliseum. The image lightens.

 35. In the Curves dialog box, select the **EYEDROPPER on the left** (the "Set Black Point" eyedropper in the lower right area of the Curves dialog box).
The image darkens a little. **Click on a dark part of the arch**.

36. In the drop down **CHANNEL:** select **GREEN**.

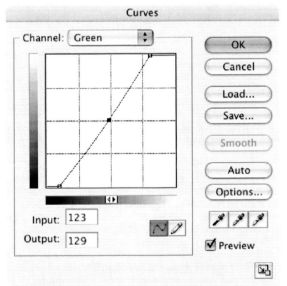

37. In the Graph area, place your cursor at the midpoint of the diagonal line and drag the line down and to the right to color correct. Look at the INPUT and OUTPUT values. Those values should be close to 123 Input and 129 Output.

38. Click OK.

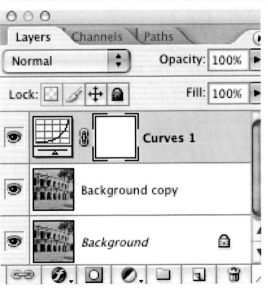

39. In your Layers Palette, you will see the Curves Adjustment layer above the Background Copy layer. Adjustment Layers affect only the layers beneath.

40. File > Save.

41. Click and hold again on the "**Create new fill or adjustment layer**" icon at the bottom of the Layers Palette and select **LEVELS**.

Levels has a histogram which allows you to slide the sliders to adjust the white point, the midtone and the black point tones in the image. If you have the Preview box checked (the default) you can see the effect on the image as you slide the sliders. Most times, you will move the white point and black point sliders towards the center.

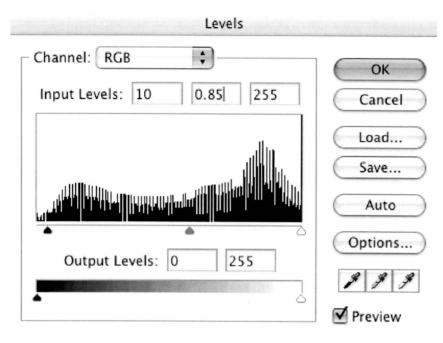

42. In the **INPUT LEVELS**: type in **10, 0.85, 255**.

43. Click OK.

44. **FILE > SAVE**.

45. Click on the **Background Copy Layer to activate it.**

46. With the **MAGIC WAND TOOL** click the sky to select it.

47. **HOLDING the SHIFT KEY**, continue clicking on the sky to select as much as you can.

48. **ACTIVATE THE LEVELS LAYER** by selecting it in the Layers Palette.

49. Click and hold again on the "**Create new fill or adjustment layer**" **icon** at the bottom of the Layers Palette and select **PHOTO FILTER**.

50. Choose "**Deep Blue**" and click OK.

The Photo Filter offers a set range of colors that can be added to an image. By selecting the sky, you have isolated

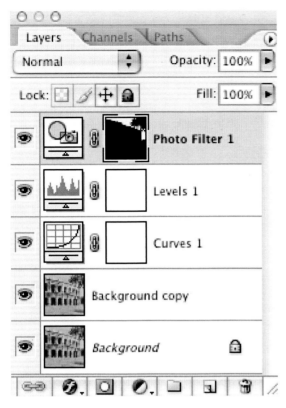

the filter to only affecting what is selected. This can be seen in the Photo Filter Adjustment Layer Mask.

51. File > Save.

52. Click and hold again on the "**Create new fill or adjustment layer" icon** ⊘. at the bottom of the Layers Palette and select **COLOR BALANCE**.

Color Balance allows you to correct color tones in highlights, midtones and shadows. You want to adjust the sliders only slightly to enhance the color. A good rule is not to adjust the sliders more than 15 in either direction. If the color cast is too green, you want to slide towards the red, etc. You will eventually train your eye for color correction. It is also good to save the document and open it at another time to look at the image with a "fresh eye."

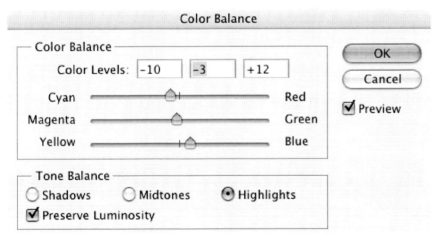

53. In the Color Balance dialog box, click on the **HIGHLIGHTS** radio button.

54. Type in: **-10, -3, +12**.

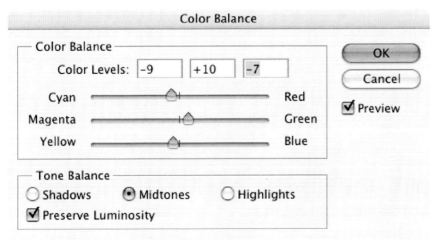

55. Click on the **MIDTONES** radio button.

56. Type in: **-9, +10, -7**.

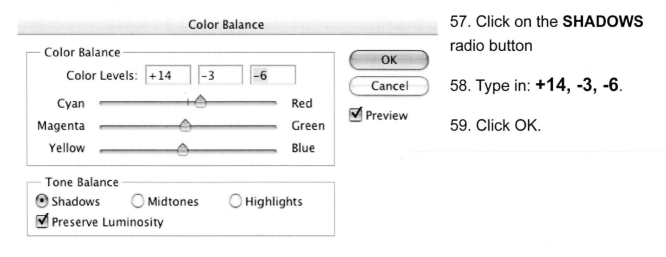

57. Click on the **SHADOWS** radio button

58. Type in: **+14, -3, -6**.

59. Click OK.

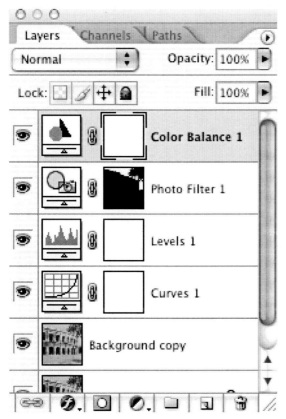

60. You can see the Color Balance layer above the others in the Layers Palette.

61. File > Save.

Photo Retouching

The next section of this workshop concentrates on retouching an image by using the Cloning Stamp Tool, the Healing Brush Tool, the Spot Healing Brush Tool and the Patch Tool.

62. **Create a new layer on top of the Color Balance layer** by clicking on the **NEW LAYER ICON** in the Layers Palette.

63. Double-click on the WORD "Layer 1" and when you get the flashing cursor, rename the layer to **REPAIR. You will make corrections only on this layer.** This gives you flexibility to erase on the layer if you do not like the repairs.

64. Click on the **Zoom Tool** in your Tool Box and zoom into the sky area in the photo. You want the zoom percentage to be 100% .

65. Click on the **Cloning Stamp** Tool in your Toolbox.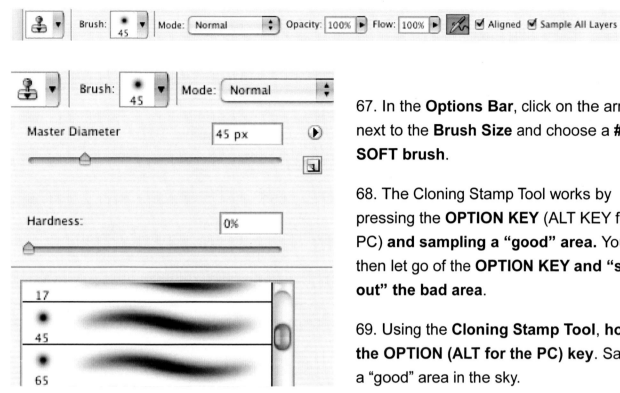

66. In the **Options Bar**, click on the box next to "**SAMPLE ALL LAYERS**" to check it.

67. In the **Options Bar**, click on the arrow next to the **Brush Size** and choose a **#45 SOFT brush**.

68. The Cloning Stamp Tool works by pressing the **OPTION KEY** (ALT KEY for the PC) **and sampling a "good" area.** You will then let go of the **OPTION KEY and "stamp out" the bad area**.

69. Using the **Cloning Stamp Tool**, **hold the OPTION (ALT for the PC) key**. Sample a "good" area in the sky.

70. Let go of the **OPTION KEY** and click on the "Bad" area in the **Sky** to paste.

You will continue to "Sample" the "good area" with your OPTION KEY and paste letting go of the OPTION KEY to click the mouse on the area to be cloned. You will see a cross-hair icon as you "paste" using the Cloning Stamp. Be careful to watch the cross-hair as you stamp. Sometimes you may get unwanted "pasting" if you do not continually resample.

71. **FILE > SAVE.**

72. Using the Clone Stamp Tool, use the same methods above to "clone out" the bad areas. With any of the Brush Tools, hit the **[(left bracket) Key to make the Brush smaller** and the **] (right bracket) Key to make the Brush larger**.

73. **Continue using the Cloning Stamp Tool to repair the spots and specks.**

74. File > Save periodically.

The Spot Healing Brush Tool and the Healing Brush Tool

The Spot Healing Brush  is the default brush for the group of Healing Tools. It is very easy to use. You simply click on the spot you wish to repair and it "heals." It is not quite as adaptable as the Healing Brush Tool, however, as it does not give as many options. Generally use the "Proximity Match" mode. This tool is good for small areas.

75. Click on the **Spot Healing Brush Tool** in your Toolbox.

76. In the **Options Bar**, click on the box next to "**SAMPLE ALL LAYERS**" to check it.

77. **Holding the SPACEBAR, and PAN down** to the Coliseum.

78. **Zoom in to the very bottom left archway.**

79. Using the Spot Healing Brush, click on several of the white spots to get rid of them.

The **Healing Brush** may also be used on the Repair layer. It is located under the Spot Healing Brush. The **Healing Brush** is similar to the Cloning Stamp in that it clones pixels from selected areas to cover up damaged areas but the Healing Brush also takes into consideration the tonality and the texture of the surrounding pixels in the area to be corrected.

Click and hold on the Spot Healing Brush Tool in your Toolbox to select the Healing Brush.

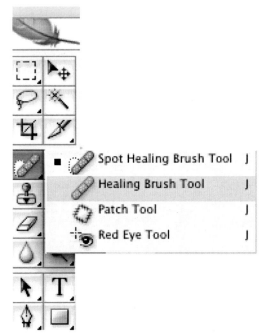

80. In the **Options Bar,** Click on the Brush Size to choose a **25 diameter brush**. Slide the **Hardness** slider down to **0 (zero)** to make it a soft brush.

81. In the **Options Bar**, click on the box next to "**SAMPLE ALL LAYERS**" to check it.

82. Hold the **OPTION KEY**.

83. In the photo, **click and sample a "good" area** in the photo.

84. Let go of the **OPTION KEY** and click on a white spot to "paste" and cover the bad area.

85. Carefully continue to sample the good area of the image with the OPTION KEY and paste to the bad area to cover up the spots and bad areas.

86. **File > Save**.

The Patch Tool

The **Patch Tool** takes texture, light and shading of the area to be repaired into account by using a "patch" to cover the imperfection in the photo. With the Patch Tool, you will **make a selection of the "bad" area and drag it to a "good" area to "Patch" the damaged area.**

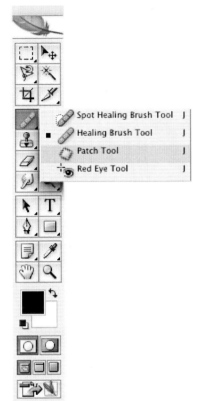

87. In your Tool Box, **click and hold on the Healing Brush** to get the **Patch Tool**.

88. You must be on the **BACKGROUND COPY** layer to use the Patch Tool. Click on the **BACKGROUND COPY** layer in the Layers palette to activate that layer.

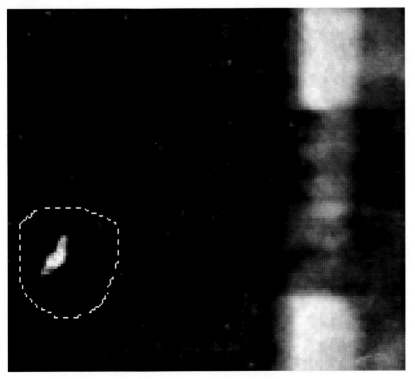

89. Keep the Default settings in the Options Bar. With the Patch Tool, **click and hold the mouse** and carefully **circle the large white spot in the lower left archway**.

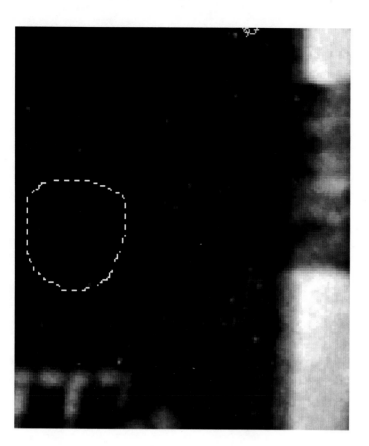

90. Click and hold inside of the selection and drag to a "good" area in the sheet.

91. DESELECT (Command + D for the Mac or Control + D for the PC).

92. Pan over to another large spot on the image. Circle the another "bad" area with the **Patch Tool** and drag to a "good" area time. Continue using the Patch Tool to repair the larger spots.

93. **File > Save**.

94. **Click on the REPAIR layer to activate it**.

95. Using the **Healing Brush** 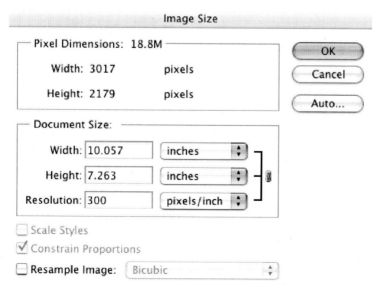 again, repair other areas in the photo. You may also want to use the **Cloning Stamp** again. You can press and **hold on the SPACE BAR while holding the Mouse** to move to other areas of the photo without changing Tools.

96. After healing and cloning bad areas, **FILE > SAVE**.

You may close the photo.

97. **Open > Young Boy.tif from your folder.**

98. IMAGE > IMAGE SIZE.

99. Type in "**300**" for the **resolution**. Make sure the RESAMPLE IMAGE box is **NOT** checked. Notice that the Width and Height in inches increases proportionately.

100. Using the **Crop Tool** , crop the photo to get rid of some of the background area. This will give more of a close-up of the young boy.

101. Hit the RETURN / ENTER KEY to make the crop take effect.

102. **File > Save As > Young Boy. PSD.**

103. Create a duplicate layer.

104. **FILTER > SHARPEN > UNSHARP MASK**.

105. The **Unsharp Mask** dialog box opens. You will enter the same values as before. Both images were shot originally using 35 mm film - so the same setting will work here.

106. Enter **100 in the AMOUNT** field, **4.0 in the RADIUS** field and a **THRESHOLD of 1.**

107. Click OK.

108. FILE > SAVE.

109. **FILTER > NOISE > DESPECKLE**. This will take out some of the graininess of the photo.

110. **Add a Curves Adjustment Layer**.

   The **RED Channel:** Input 134; Output 123

   The **GREEN Channel:** Input 144; Output 115

   The **BLUE Channel:** Input 140; Output 123

111. File > Save.

112. Add a New Layer. Name it "Repair."

113. **Using your Healing Brush, and Cloning Stamp Tool, repair any spots or specks on the REPAIR layer.**

114. When you are finished repairing the image, SAVE and close the document.

Repairing Black and White Images

115. Open Baby.jpg.

116. **Crop** the image to get rid of the excess area.

117. Hit the RETURN / ENTER KEY to make the crop take effect.

118. Create a **DUPLICATE LAYER**.

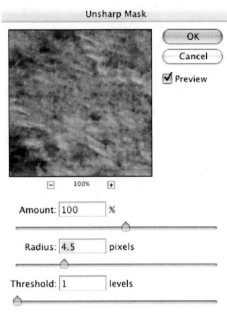

119. Apply **UNSHARP MASK**.

120. Click OK.

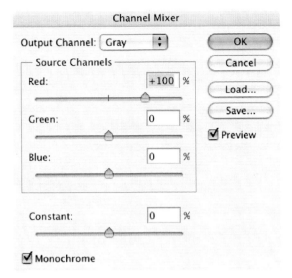

121. Create a **CHANNEL MIXER** Adjustment Layer.

122. Click on the **MONOCHROME** box to take the colors out of the image.

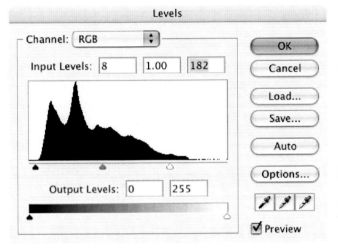

123. Create a **LEVELS** Adjustment Layer.

124. Slide the sliders to read in the **Input Levels: 8, 1.00, 182.**

125. Click OK.

126. Create a New Layer by clicking on the **NEW LAYER ICON** on the Layers palette.

127. Double click on the **WORD Layer 1** and rename the Layer **REPAIR**.

128. Zoom into the photo by using the **Zoom Tool**.

129. File > Save As > Baby.PSD (Photoshop document).

130. Using your **Healing Brush Tool and Cloning Stamp Tool**, repair the damaged areas. **Make sure you stay on the Repair Layer**.

131. When finished, FILE >SAVE.

You may close this document.

You have completed this tutorial.

Remember to drag your desktop folder to your USB Flash Drive or burn on a CD.

Photoshop Tutorial

Workshop 6 – Type and Layer Effects

OBJECTIVE: After completing this Workshop Tutorial, you will be able to use the Horizontal Type Tool to create vector type. You will learn how to warp and rasterize type. You will use the Horizontal Type Mask Tool and place an image inside the text. Finally, you will learn how to create a Duotone and combine a grayscale image with a color image.

Create a folder on your desktop and name it "Photoshop Tutorial 6." Save all files during the Workshop to this folder. At the end of this tutorial, drag your desktop folder to your USB Flash Drive or burn on a CD.

DRAG TO YOUR DESKTOP FOLDER FROM YOUR CD: "Photoshop Tutorial 6 Images"

Using the Horizontal Type Tool

Type in Photoshop® is vector-based. This means it is editable type. You can change the font, the size, the style, the color, etc, just as you would be able to in an vector-based program such as Adobe Illustrator®. In order to apply a Photoshop® specific effect, you will have to rasterize the type.

1. Open Ivy.jpg.

2. Command + 0 (zero) for the Mac or Control + 0 for the PC to **Fit In Screen**.

3. Select the **HORIZONTAL TYPE TOOL** T from the Toolbox.

4. Click on the Ivy image with the Horizontal Type Tool (DO NOT DRAG - just click) and type the word **Nature**.

5. In the Layers Palette, you will see a **TYPE LAYER**.

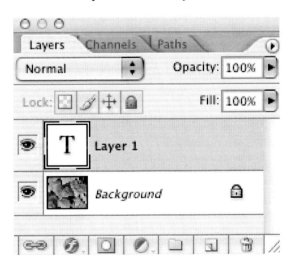

6. **DOUBLE-CLICK** the word Nature to select the word.

7. In the **OPTIONS BAR**, select a **font** of your choice.

8. In the **OPTIONS BAR**, select drop-down menu next to the 𝕋 symbol and select **72 pt**.

9. You can also type in the size you want. **Type in 100** in the size field.

10. To choose a color, you need to click on the **COLOR SWATCH** in the Options Bar.

Color Swatch

11. When you click on the COLOR SWATCH, the **COLOR PICKER** opens up. You must click on a color in the rainbow strip to choose a different color, then choose a value of that color in the large square.

12. If you **take the CURSOR outside of the Color Picker box**, you can select a color from the image itself. The cursor will turn into the EYEDROPPER to sample the image color, in this case.

13. Click **OK**.

14. Using the **MOVE TOOL**, 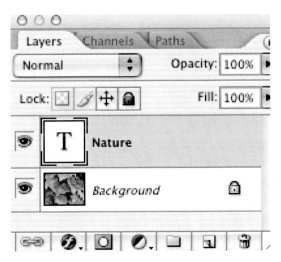 move the word Nature to center the word near the top of the image.

15. The Type Layer now has the word "Nature" as the name of the layer.

16. FILE > SAVE AS > **Type.PSD**

17. To space out the lettering, you can use the **TRACKING** option in the Character Palette. **WINDOW > CHARACTER**.

18. Select the TYPE TOOL and **double-Click the word Nature** to select the word.

19. In the Character Palette, click on the drop down arrow in the **Tracking field and select 100**. The type spreads out.

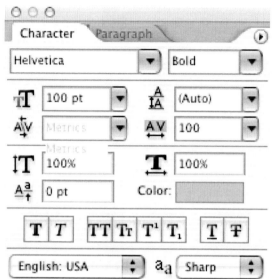

20. Click on the drop down arrow again and take the Tracking of the type back to 0.

AV 0

21. To **KERN** type, place your type cursor between the letters "u" and "r." Kerning affects the space between **only TWO letters of type**, whereas **Tracking affects the entire selection of type**. AV Metrics

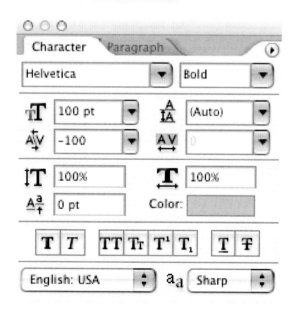

22. Select the drop down arrow of the **KERNING** field and choose **-100.**

23. The space between the "u" and "r" has closed up.

24. In the **KERNING** field, click on the from down arrow again and choose "0" to take away the kerning effect.

25. FILE > SAVE.

Warping Type

26. Using the HORIZONTAL TYPE TOOL, double-click the word Nature to select it again.

27. In the **OPTIONS BAR**, select the **TYPE WARP** option.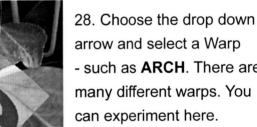

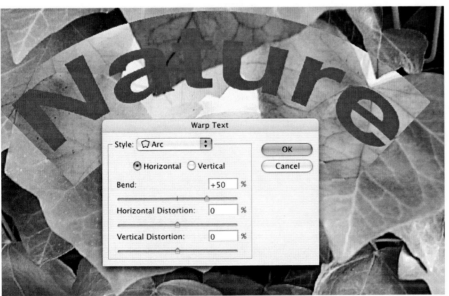

28. Choose the drop down arrow and select a Warp - such as **ARCH**. There are many different warps. You can experiment here.

29. Click OK.

Rasterizing Type

To **RASTERIZE TYPE** so that the font does not have to be downloaded when going to print - or if you want to do special Photoshop effects to the type, go under **LAYER > RASTERIZE > TYPE**. The type will no longer be editable. If the word is misspelled, you must discard the layer and re-type the word.

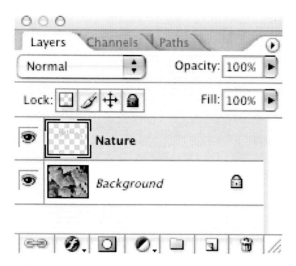

30. LAYER > RASTERIZE > TYPE. The word Nature is now rasterized. The layer is no longer a type layer but an image just like the Ivy image.

31. FILE > SAVE.

Text Boxes

To constrain text into a specific area as well as apply paragraph attributes, you need to draw a **TEXT BOX with the Horizontal Type Tool**.

32. Using the Horizontal Type Tool, **draw a box beneath the word Nature**. You are creating a text box. The words will now be constrained to the type box.

33. Change the font size to **14** in the Options Bar. Type some copy. Notice that the type is constrained to the type box.

34. Using the Horizontal Type Tool, **highlight the text in the text box**.

35. In the Options Bar, select the **COLOR SWATCH**.

36. **Choose a different color** and click OK.

37. With the text in the text box still highlighted, you will change the **LEADING** of the type. Leading controls the space between the lines of type. You must have the entire block of type highlighted to affect the leading of the entire text. If you want more space between the lines, increase the leading - and vice versa.

The Leading field looks like: 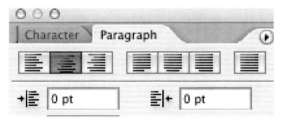 .

The default is "Auto," which is 120% of the font size. You can either type in the leading amount or use the drop down arrow. **Type in 16 in the Leading field**. The space between the lines changes.

38. Located next to the Character Palette is the Paragraph Palette. Just as with the Character Palette, most of the type options are found in the Options Bar at the top of your screen. However, it is convenient to have the Character and Paragraph palette "floating" if you need it. **Click on the PARAGRAPH PALETTE tab to bring this palette to the front**.

39. In the Paragraph Palette, you can align the type: **Left Aligned, Center Aligned, Right Aligned, Justify Last (line) Left, Justify Last (line) Right and Justify All (force justify to both right and left).** Experiment with the different alignments. When finished, go back to Left Aligned.

40. Select the **MOVE TOOL** and center the text box under the word Nature.

41. Using the **Horizontal Type Tool,** you can Warp the text box type if you wish.

42. **FILE > SAVE**.

43. With the **MOVE TOOL, activate the NATURE layer**.

44. At the bottom of the Layers Palette, **click and hold on the "Add a layer style" Icon** 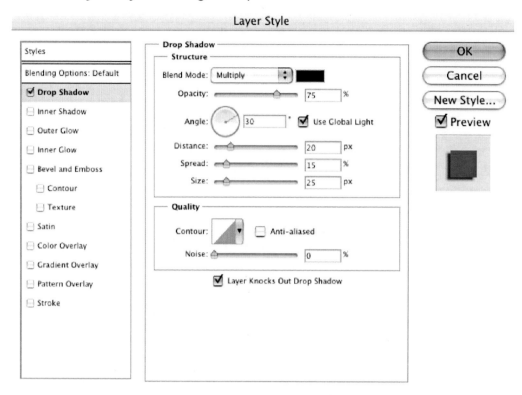.

45. Choose "**DROP SHADOW**."

46. The **Layer Styles** dialog box opens.

47. In the **ANGLE** field, type **30**.

48. In the **DISTANCE** field, type **20**.

49. In the **SPREAD** field, type **15**.

50. In the **SIZE** field, type **25**.

51. Click OK.

52. FILE > SAVE.

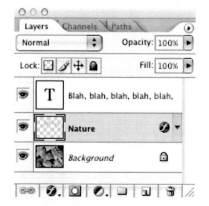

In the Layers Palette, you can see the "EFFECTS" icon attached to the Nature layer showing that there have been layer effects added.

33.33%   Doc: 14.4M/24.6M

Your finished image might look similar to the above image.

You may close this document.

Type Mask

The **Type Mask Tool** creates a selection in the form of type characters. You will be filling the Type Mask with a photograph. The TYPE MASK works best with large, bold type.

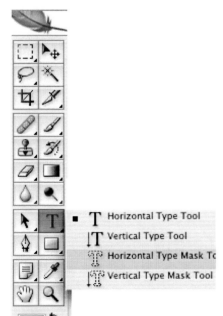

T Horizontal Type Tool
IT Vertical Type Tool
Horizontal Type Mask To
Vertical Type Mask Tool

53. Open Yellow Roses.jpg.

54. Open All Blue.jpg.

55. Activate the Yellow Roses image.

56. **Click and hold the Horizontal Type Tool** to select the **HORIZONTAL TYPE MASK TOOL**.

57. In the **OPTIONS BAR**, choose **IMPACT** as the font and **210** for the size.

58. Make sure the paragraph setting is **FLUSH LEFT**
 .

59. DOUBLE-CLICK on the Quick Mask Mode icon in the Toolbox. Select a different color for the Quick Mask Mode by clicking on the red color swatch. After you have chosen a contrasting color to yellow, click OK.

60. In the middle (vertically) and to the left (horizontally) of the Yellow Roses image, click your mouse to insert the TYPE MASK cursor.

61. In **ALL CAPS**, type the word **COLOR**. It appears as if it is a Quick Mask.

62. **Select the MOVE TOOL. The word COLOR turns into a selection.**

63. Activate the All Blue.jpg image.

64. Go under the **SELECT** menu > **SELECT ALL**.

65. **EDIT > COPY**.

66. Activate the Yellow Roses image.

67. **EDIT > PASTE INTO**.

68. On the thumbnail of the All Blue image in the Layers Palette, you can move the pasted image inside of the Type Mask (using the MOVE TOOL).

69. On the thumbnail of the Type Mask in the Layers Palette, you can move the type around.

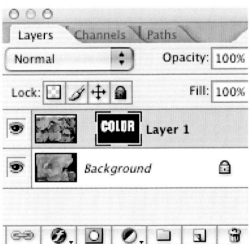

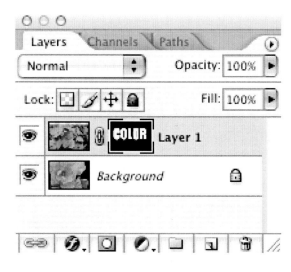

70. Click on the blank space between the two thumbnails to link the type mask with the pasted image. They will move together as long as they are linked.

71. FILE > SAVE.

72. Double-click on the word "Layer 1" and rename the layer "Type Mask."

73. At the bottom of the Layers Palette, **click and hold on the "Add a layer style" Icon.**

74. Choose "**DROP SHADOW**."

75. The **Layer Styles** dialog box opens.

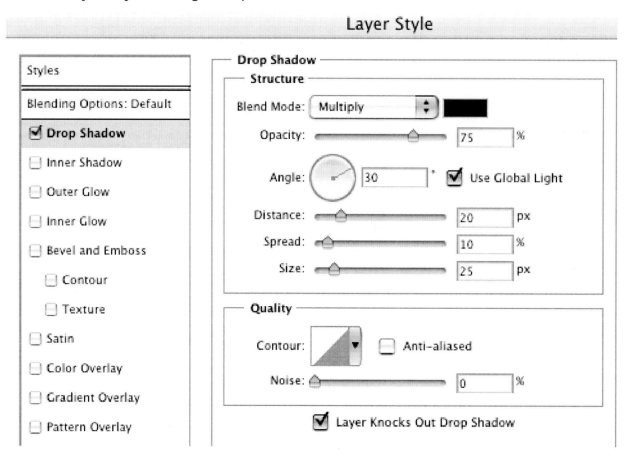

76. Enter in the **ANGLE** field, type **30**.

77. In the **DISTANCE** field, type **20**.

78. In the **SPREAD** field, type **10**.

79. In the **SIZE** field, type **25**.

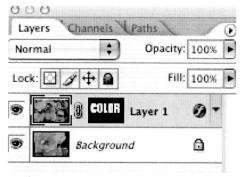

80. **Click the "Bevel and Emboss" box** in the same dialog box. **Double-click** on the word "Bevel and Emboss" so that menu appears in the dialog box.

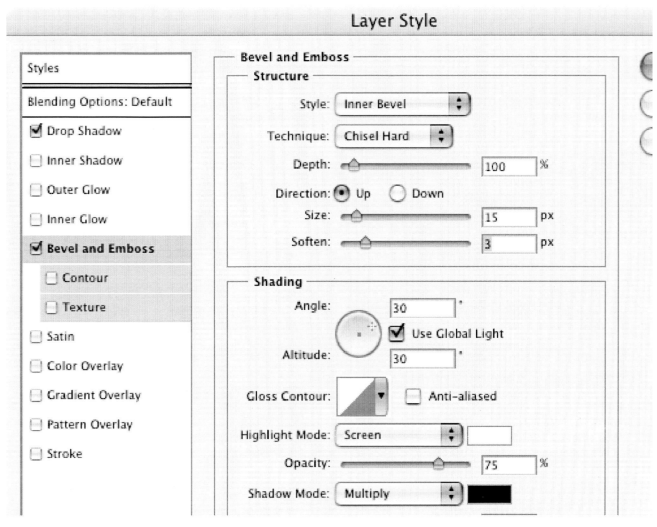

81. **Enter the settings:**

Style: Inner Bevel

Technique: Chisel Hard

Direction: Up

Size: 15 px

Soften: 3 px

Angle: 30

82. Click **OK**.

83. **File > Save**.

You may close this document.

Creating a Duotone

A **Duotone** is typically a 2-color photograph. In Photoshop, a Duotone is classified as a Monotone (1 color), a Duotone (2 color), a Tritone (3 color) or a Quadtone (4 color). Duotones are located in the Duotone Options dialog box after you convert a photo into a grayscale.

84. **Open > Hostas.jpg**.

You will need to convert this image into a grayscale before creating the Duotone.

85. Go under **IMAGE > MODE > LAB COLOR**.

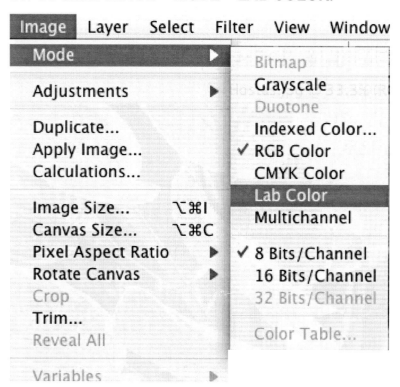

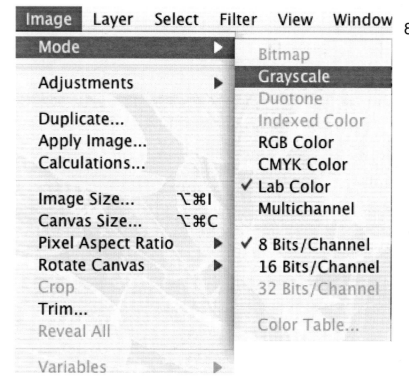

86. **IMAGE > MODE > GRAYSCALE**.

87. Click **OK** to discard color information.

88. Go under **IMAGE > MODE > DUOTONE**.

The **DUOTONE OPTIONS** dialog box appears.

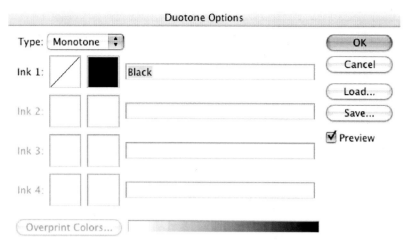

89. Click on the **BLACK COLOR SQUARE**.

90. Click the **COLOR LIBRARIES** button.

91. Make sure that "**PANTONE SOLID COATED**" is the Color Library chosen.

92. Pantone® Matching System colors are used for commercial printing. They are used for spot color printing as well as for printing jobs that have less that 4-colors. If the job has 4 or more colors, CMYK is used.

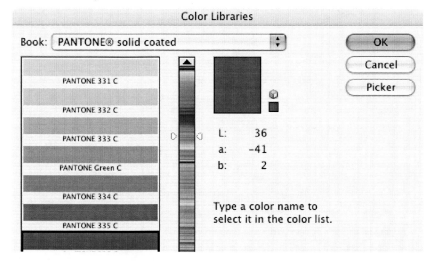

93. You can either type in a Pantone number (If you know of one) in your number pad on the keyboard or scroll through the swatches. **TYPE IN 336** to go to that color.

94. Click the OK button in the Color Libraries dialog box.

95. Click the OK button in the Duotone Options dialog box.

The Hostas turn green.

95. Go under **IMAGE > MODE > DUOTONE** again.

96. This time, click on the down arrow next to **TYPE: and choose DUOTONE**.

97. Click on the **WHITE** color swatch to choose a second color.

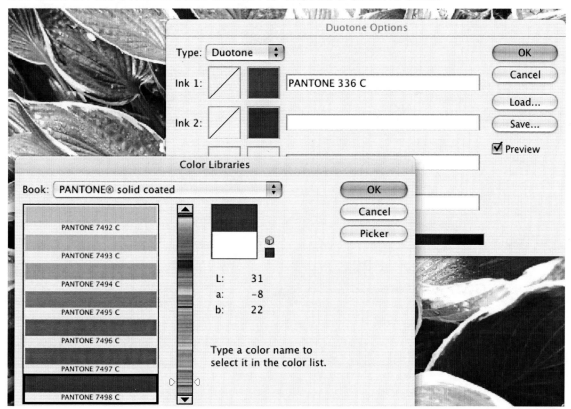

The preview of the image turns into a Duotone.

98. Click the OK button in the Color Libraries dialog box.

99. Click the OK button in the Duotone Options dialog box.

100. **FILE > SAVE AS > DUOTONE**.

You will convert the image back to RGB mode so that you can combine color images with a grayscale.

101. **IMAGE > MODE > RGB**.

102. Using the **Horizontal Type Tool**, click on the upper portion of the image.

103. In your **OPTIONS BAR**, change the font size to **48 pt**. Leave the font at **IMPACT**.

104. Type "**Great Plants for Your Garden**."

105. Highlight the text with your **Type Tool**.

106. Click the **COLOR SWATCH** in the Options Bar.

107. In the Color Picker Dialog box, choose the **Color Libraries** button again.

108. Choose **116C** as the color.

109. Click OK.

110. Select the **MOVE TOOL**.

111. Using the MOVE TOOL, center the headline and move it towards the top of the image.

112. **FILE > OPEN (or BROWSE) > Yellow Flowers.jpg**.

113. Drag the Yellow Flowers.jpg document into the Duotone document.

114. **EDIT > TRANSFORM > SCALE**.

115. Holding the Shift Key, drag the top right corner to scale the photo proportionately.

116. **FILE > SAVE AS > Garden Poster.PSD**.

117. In the Layers Palette, double-click on the WORD Layer 1. Rename the layer "Yellow Flowers."

118. Using the MOVE TOOL, drag the Yellow Flowers layer to the right side of the image - lined up flushed right, underneath the headline.

119. Open > White Flowers.jpg.

120. Using the MOVE TOOL, drag the White Flowers image into the Garden Poster document.

121. **EDIT > TRANSFORM > SCALE**.

122. Holding the Shift Key, drag the top right corner to scale the photo proportionately. You may have to reduce the VIEWING SIZE of the document to see the edges of the transformation handles.

123. **FILE > SAVE**.

124. Using the MOVE TOOL, drag the new layer image under the Yellow Flower image in the document.

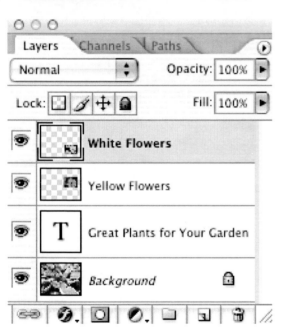

125. In the Layers Palette, rename Layer 1 to White Flowers.

126. **Open > Red Roses.jpg**.

127. **Drag the Red Roses image into the Garden Poster document**.

128. **Scale** the Red Roses image to be the same size as the other two flower images (EDIT > TRANSFORM > SCALE).

129. Proportionately scale the Red Roses image down to the same size as the other two images.

130. Move the new layer over to the left side of the document. Move it towards the bottom of the document - lined up with the White Flowers.

131. Name the new layer "Red Roses."

132. FILE > SAVE.

Linking Layers

If you wish to affect several layers at once, you can link the layers. As an example, if you believe the flowers are all too large, you can link all three layers before you scale the layers and all three layers will scale at once.

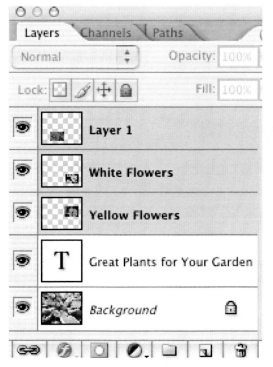

133. In the Layers Palette, press and **HOLD the Shift Key** and click on the three flowers layers to select the layers in the Layers Palette.

134. Now, click on the **LINK ICON** in the bottom of the Layers Palette. All three layers are linked.

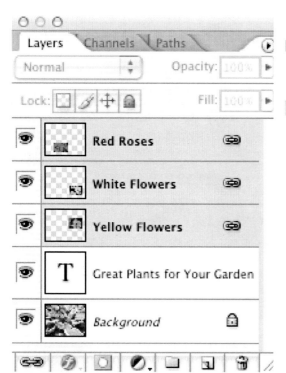

135. Using the **MOVE TOOL**, move the layers to the left to center under the type headline.

136. **UNLINK** the Layers by clicking on the LINK ICON again.

137. Your composite should look similar to this example.

138. **FILE > SAVE**.

139. Open **Butterfly Bush**.jpg.

140. Drag the Butterfly Bush image into the Garden Poster document.

141. Scale the new layer to match the other three flower images.

142. Name the new layer "Butterfly Bush."

144. Shift + Click on the Red Roses layer and the White Flowers Layer in your Layers Palette to select the layers.

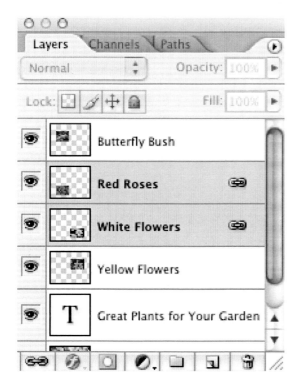

145. Click the **LINK ICON** to link the Layers.

146. In the **OPTIONS BAR**, click the **ALIGNED TOP EDGES ICON**.

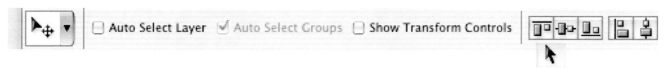

147. The top edges of the two layers align at the top. Click the **LINK ICON** again to **UNLINK** the two layers.

148. **Shift + Click the Butterfly Bush Layer and the Yellow Flowers Layer to select both of those Layers**.

149. Click the **LINK ICON** to link the Layers.

150. In the **OPTIONS BAR**, click the **ALIGNED TOP EDGES ICON.**

151. FILE > SAVE.

152. Select the **HORIZONTAL TYPE TOOL** .

153. **Highlight the headline to select it.**

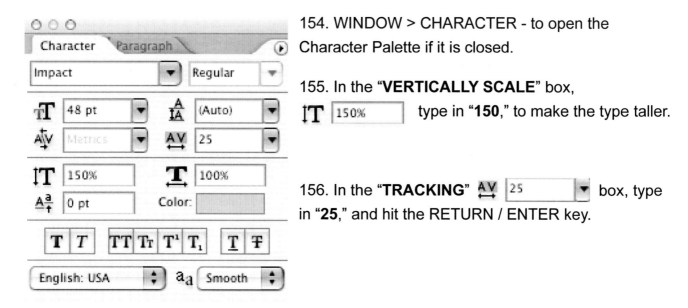

154. WINDOW > CHARACTER - to open the Character Palette if it is closed.

155. In the "**VERTICALLY SCALE**" box, type in "**150**," to make the type taller.

156. In the "**TRACKING**" box, type in "**25**," and hit the RETURN / ENTER key.

157. Using the **MOVE TOOL**, center the headline between the left and right edges of the document.

158. FILE > SAVE.

159. Click on the Type Layer to activate it.

160. Add a **DROP SHADOW TO THE HEADLINE**.

Copying Layer Styles

You can easily copy Layer Styles from one layer to another by using the CONTROL KEY on the Mac OR the RIGHT MOUSE BUTTON on the PC.

161. Either **CONTROL + CLICK** (Mac) **or** use the **RIGHT MOUSE BUTTON** (PC) on the TYPE LAYER to get a submenu.

Layer Properties...
Blending Options...

Duplicate Layer...
Delete Layer

Group into New Smart Object

Link Layers
Select Linked Layers

Select Similar Layers

Rasterize Type
Create Work Path
Convert to Shape

Horizontal
Vertical

Anti-Alias None
Anti-Alias Sharp
Anti-Alias Crisp
Anti-Alias Strong
Anti-Alias Smooth

Convert To Paragraph Text

Warp Text...

Copy Layer Style
Paste Layer Style
▼

162. Click "**COPY LAYER STYLE**."

163. Click on the **Yellow Flowers Layer** and either CONTROL + CLICK (Mac) or use the RIGHT MOUSE BUTTON (PC) to get a **submenu**.

164. Click "**PASTE LAYER STYLE**."

The DROP SHADOW from the Type Layer is repeated on the Yellow Roses Layer.

165. **Repeat the "PASTE LAYER STYLE" for the other three layers with the flowers.**

166. FILE > SAVE.

You may close the document.

You have finished this Workshop Tutorial.

Remember to drag your desktop folder to your USB Flash Drive or burn on a CD.

Photoshop Tutorial

Workshop 7 – Surrealistic Composite Images

OBJECTIVE: After completing this Workshop Tutorial, you will be able to use a variety of methods to create surrealistic composite images in Adobe Photoshop® . You will be learning how to use Layer Masks, Blending Modes and Gradient Grayscale Masks to create a surrealistic composite photo.

Create a folder on your desktop and name it "Photoshop Tutorial 7." Save all files during the Workshop to this folder. At the end of this tutorial, drag your desktop folder to your USB Flash Drive or burn on a CD.

DRAG TO YOUR DESKTOP FOLDER FROM YOUR CD: "Photoshop Tutorial 7 Images"

A surrealistic image is an image that is dream-like. Visual imagery can be used in a way to create composite images to reflect the subconscious thoughts. Even though the photographs are real, the surrealistic imagery is combined in such a way that the composite concept is not logical.

A **Blending Mode** combines pixels together with the layers beneath. Examples of Blending Modes include: screen, dissolve, multiply, overlay, hard light, soft light, color dodge, color burn, darken, lighten, difference, exclusion, hue, saturation, color and luminosity. Blending Modes are found in the Layers Palette, the Options Bar and under Layer Styles.

A **Layer Mask** hides or reveals parts of a layer. You can apply as many layer masks as you wish but only one at a time. You must <u>apply</u> the mask before adding another Layer Mask.

1. Open Adobe Photoshop®.

2. **Open Sky.jpg, Shutters.jpg and Steel.jpg documents.**

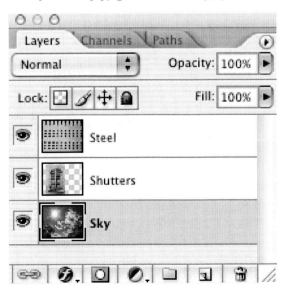

3. Make the **SKY image** your **Background layer**. You will drag and drop Shutters and Steel into this photograph.

4. Using the **MOVE tool**, drag Shutters into the Sky document.

5. **Activate the Steel** photo, using the **MOVE** tool, drag Steel into the Sky document.

6. Make sure that **Shutters** image is the Layer on top of Sky.

7. The Steel image needs to be the top Layer.

8. **Name the Layers:** Steel, Shutters and Sky.

9. **FILE > SAVE AS > SURREALISM.PSD**

10. Turn the **EYE ICON** of the Steel Layer off to hide the Layer.

11. Activate the Shutters Layer.

12. **Edit > Transform > Flip Horizontal**.

13. **FILE > SAVE**.

You will now add a **Layer Mask** to the Shutters Layer.

14. Click on the **Layer Mask Icon** on the bottom of the Layers palette.

15. Hit the "D" Key to get the Default Colors in the Color Swatches in the Toolbox.

16. Hit the "X" Key to switch the Foreground and Background colors (to make Black the Foreground Color in this case).

A Layer Mask will hide or reveal parts of the layer. You can use the Brush Tool with a soft edge to fade the layer. If you use a hard brush, it acts like an eraser. Black will take the layer image away and white will add the layer image back.

17. Using the **BRUSH TOOL** and a **Hard brush**, (**Black needs to be the foreground color**) paint out the wall and background around the Shutters. **Leave the brick border around the Shutters.**

The Layer Mask shows the hidden part of the Shutters image covered in black.

18. The image no longer has a background behind the Shutters but the brick border around the Shutters is still there..

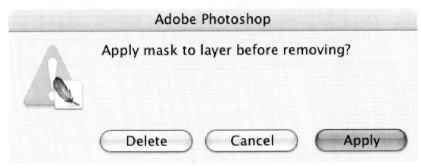

19. After the background around the Shutters is gone, **drag the Layer Mask icon into the Layers Trash Can** and **APPLY** the Layer Mask.

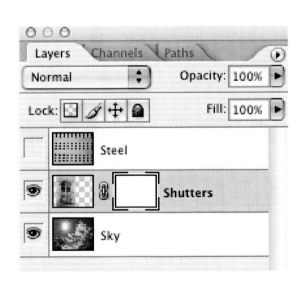

20. **Add another Layer mask** to the Shutters Layer.

21. In the Toolbox, select the **GRADIENT TOOL** .

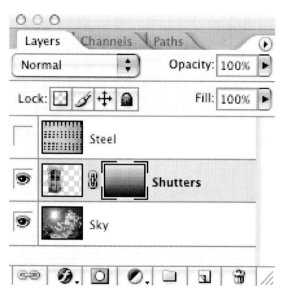

22. Using the **GRADIENT TOOL, drag a gradient on the Shutters** (making sure you are **on the Layer Mask**). Drag the gradient from BELOW the bottom of the Shutters to ABOVE the Shutters.

23. Using the **BRUSH TOOL**, (with a large, **SOFT BRUSH - #100** and **BLACK** as foreground color) paint out extra areas on the **same LAYER MASK** of the Shutters Layer (as shown in the above photo).

24. Use **WHITE as a Foreground Color to add** any areas of the Shutters image back

25. **FILE > SAVE**.

26. **Turn on the Steel Layer** (click on the EYE ICON on the Layer).

27. Make sure you have the Steel Layer activated (you are on the Steel Layer).

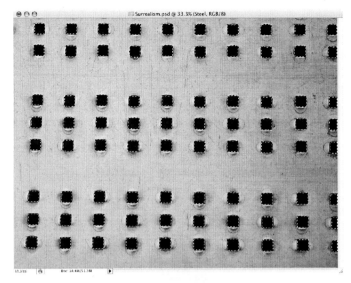

28. Using the **MAGIC WAND TOOL** 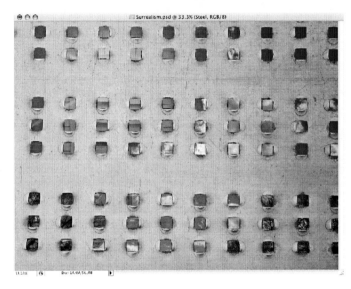, select the top black square on the Steel.

29. **HOLDING the SHIFT KEY**, select ALL of the small black squares on the Steel Layer.

30. After all of the black squares are selected, hit the **DELETE KEY** to make the black disappear so that you can see through the squares.

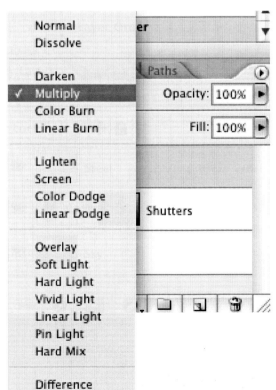

31. Click on the **Layers Blending Mode Drop Down List** and choose a **MULTIPLY** for the Steel Layer (where it says "Normal").

32. **Experiment with different BLENDING MODES**.

33. You may also choose a **Blending Mode** in the **Option Toolbar with the Paint Brush**, choose a foreground color and "paint" areas of the photo to give additional surrealistic effects.

Your finished surrealistic composite should look similar to the image below.

34. **FILE > SAVE**. You may close this document. **You will begin a new Surrealism**.

35. Open > Field.jpg.

36. Open > Hinge.jpg.

37. Open > Rocks.jpg.

38. Make the Field.jpg the document that the other images are copied into. Name the *Background* layer FIELD.

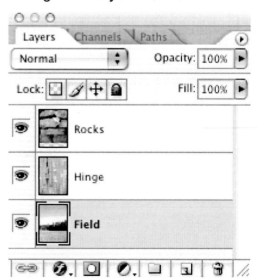

39. Using the **MOVE TOOL**, drag the Hinge into the Field document. Name the new layer HINGE.

40. Using the **MOVE TOOL** again, drag the Rocks into the Field document. Name the new layer ROCKS.

41. The Field should be the bottom layer, the Hinge in the middle layer and the Rocks should be on the top layer. Make sure you line the photos up so that they are flush top to bottom and left to right.

42. **File > Save As > Surrealism 2.PSD**.

43. Turn the EYE ICON 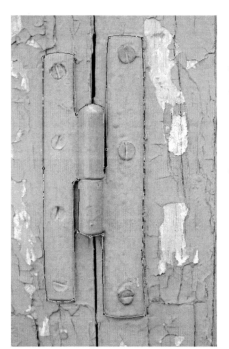 off of the Rocks layer to hide the layer.

44. Activate the Hinge layer.

Clipping Mask

A **CLIPPING MASK** groups two layers together and the bottom layer shows through the top layer. It is especially useful if you have a shape and you would like to place an image inside of a shape. The end result is similar to a Layer Mask except that the linked images are on separate layers. To use a CLIPPING MASK, the shape must be filled and must be on the bottom layer of the two. You may go under the Layer Menu > Create Clipping Mask. The Keyboard Shortcut for this is holding the OPTION / ALT KEY and clicking BETWEEN the two layers in the Layers Palette (you must hold the Option/Alt Key and click on the LINE between the two layers). The top layer will then indent in the Layers Palette.

45. Using the **PEN TOOL** (make sure that PATHS is the selected option), trace the hinge in the Hinge layer.

46. Using the **DIRECT SELECTION TOOL**, modify the points on the path to fit the hinge.

47. In the Paths Palette, save the *Work Path* as **"HINGE."**

48. FILE > SAVE.

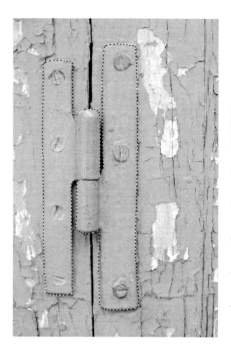

49. Load the Hinge path as a **selection** (Command + Click on the path in the Paths Palette or for the PC, Control + Click).

50. Layer Via Copy (Command + J for the Mac or Control + J for the PC).

51. The Hinge is pasted onto a new layer.

52. Name the layer "Hinge 1."

53. FILE > SAVE.

54. Activate the Hinge layer.

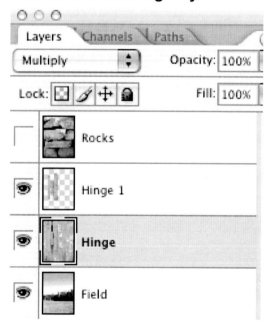

55. On the Hinge layer, click on the **Blending Mode** drop down list and choose **MULTIPLY**.

56. The layer now has a transparency to see the Field layer beneath.

57. Drag the Hinge 1 layer to the top of the layer stack in the Layers Palette.

58. Turn the EYE ICON on in the Rocks layer.

59. Make the OPACITY of the Rocks layer 25%.

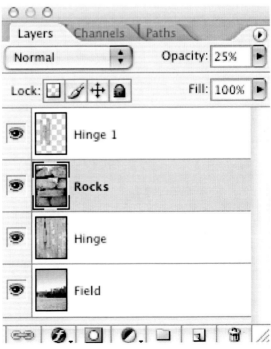

60. Click on the Field layer to activate it.

61. **Layer Via Copy**.

62. Drag the Field Copy layer to the top of the layer stack in the Layers Palette.

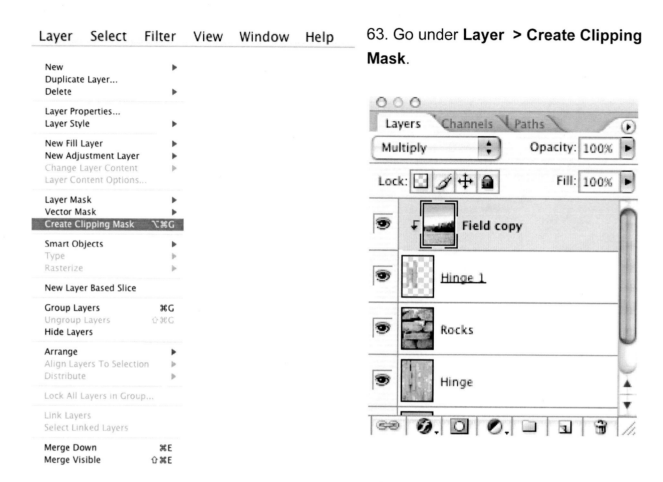

63. Go under **Layer > Create Clipping Mask**.

64. On the **Field layer**, click and hold the **Blending Mode** drop down list and choose **MULTiPLY**.

Applying Layer Styles

In the Layer Styles dialog box, you can apply many effects to the layers. The effect you will be using in this tutorial is **DROP SHADOW**.

65. Activate the Hinge 1 layer.

66. At the bottom of the Layers Palette, **click and hold on the "Add a layer style" Icon**.

67. Choose "**DROP SHADOW**."

68. The **Layer Styles** dialog box opens.

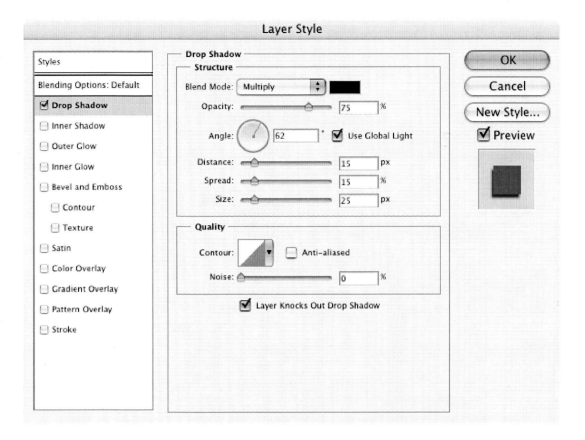

69. In the **ANGLE** field, type **62**.

70. In the **DISTANCE** field, type **15**.

71. In the **SPREAD** field, type **15**.

72. In the **SIZE** field, type **25**.

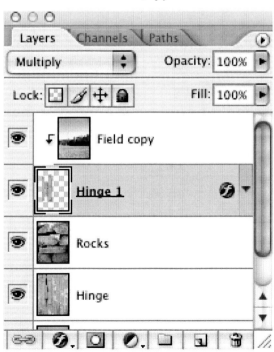

73. CLICK OK.

You can see the drop shadow effect icon on the Hinge 1 Layer.

74. With the Hinge 1 layer still activated, apply a **MULTIPLY Blending Mode** on the layer.

75. **FILE > SAVE**.

29.36%   Doc: 14.4M/73.0M

You may close the document.

You have finished this Workshop Tutorial.

Remember to drag your desktop folder to your USB Flash Drive or burn on a CD.

Photoshop Tutorial

Workshop 8 – Odds & Ends and Special Effects

OBJECTIVE: After completing this Workshop Tutorial, you will be able to use the Background Eraser Tool to erase the background of an image and use Variations to globally correct color. You will use Actions to record steps of commands that you use frequently. You will learn how to convert the Actions into a Droplet. To finish the Workshop, you will prepare your images for output for print and on the web.

Create a folder on your desktop and name it "Photoshop Tutorial 8." Save all files during the Workshop to this folder. At the end of this tutorial, drag your desktop folder to your USB Flash Drive or burn on a CD.

DRAG TO YOUR DESKTOP FOLDER FROM YOUR CD: "Photoshop Tutorial 8 Images"

Using the Background Eraser Tool

The Background Eraser Tool takes a background and erases to transparent pixels. It erasers by color and tonal values of the pixels you have targeted with the tool. It is similar to the Magic Wand in how it selects pixels to be erased. You can control the range of color pixels erased by setting the Tolerance in the Options Bar.

1. Open > Two Towers.jpg.

2. Open > Sky.jpg.

3. Using the **MOVE TOOL, drag the Sky image into the Two Towers image**.

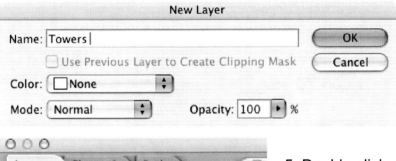

4. Double-click the *Background* layer and name the layer "Towers."

5. Double-click on the WORD Layer 1 and rename the layer "Sky."

6. Drag the Sky layer BELOW the Towers layer in the Layers Palette.

7. FILE > SAVE AS > Towers.PSD.

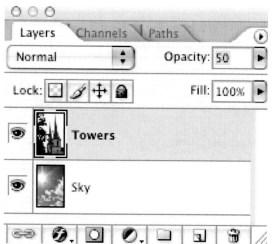

8. Take the OPACITY of the Towers layer down to 50% so that the Sky layer shows through.

9. Make sure the Sky layer is positioned in a way that it fits the height of the Towers layer. You are going to replace the gray sky of the Towers layer with the blue sky of the sky layer.

10. After you are satisfied with the positioning of the layers, bring the OPACITY of the Towers layer back to 100%.

11. **Activate the Towers layer in the Layers Palette**.

12. In the Toolbox, click and **HOLD on the ERASER TOOL** to select the **BACKGROUND ERASER**.

13. In the **OPTIONS BAR**, choose **150** as the **BRUSH SIZE**. Leave the other defaults.

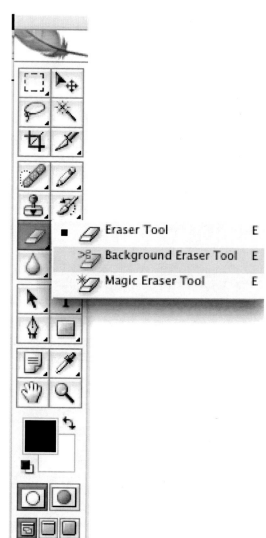

14. Using the **BACKGROUND ERASER**, use the **CROSS HAIR TARGET** ⊕ of the tool and click on the gray sky area of the Towers layer. The area you have clicked on with the Background Eraser Tool, disappears to show the blue Sky layer beneath.

15. FILE > SAVE.

16. Continue to click on the gray sky area of the TOWERS layer exposing the bright blue Sky layer beneath. **MAKE SURE THE CROSS-HAIR TARGET ONLY HITS THE GRAY SKY AREA, NOT THE BUILDINGS OR THE TREE IN THE FOREGROUND.** However, don't worry about filling in the cross on the flag.

17. Make sure you **ZOOM** into the image to make accurate erasures.

18. You can make the **BACKGROUND ERASER Brush size larger or smaller if you need to.**

19. **Make sure you erase all gray sky areas between the leaves on the tree in the foreground to expose the bright blue sky beneath.**

Your progression should look like the image below.

20. This will take a while to erase all of the dull, gray sky of the Towers layer and expose the bright, blue sky of the Sky layer.

21. If you accidentally click on the leaves of the tree, the effect will not be correct. In this case, EDIT > UNDO to undo the mistake. **BE PATIENT AND ZOOM WAY IN TO SEE THE LEAVES CLOSELY - TO MAKE SURE YOU ARE ONLY CLICKING ON THE GRAY SKY**.

22. When you finish replacing the dull sky, you will notice that the cross on the Swiss flag between the towers has turned blue.

23. Zoom into the Swiss flag.

24. Using the **PEN TOOL** and the **PATHS OPTION**, trace the cross in the middle of the Swiss flag. **REMEMBER TO CLICK AND DRAG** the Pen Tool because the flag is curved. Edit with the Direct Selection Tool.

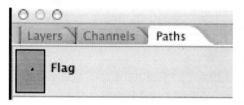

25. Save the Path as FLAG.

26. **Load the Path as a SELECTION** (Command + Click on the Path for the Mac OR Control + Click on the Path for the PC).

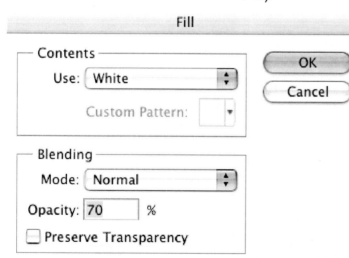

27. Edit > Fill.

28. Chose **White** in the drop-down list next to **USE:**.

29. Under **BLENDING**, make the **OPACITY 70%**.

30. The cross on the flag fills with the 70% white color.

31. Deselect.

32. **File > Save**.

Using Defringe

To make a smoother edge between the Towers layer and the Sky layer, you will use the **DEFRINGE** command under the Layers Menu. Many times when objects on layers are selected and the background is removed, there are edges left that are too sharp and make the composite look unnatural. Using DEFRINGE will help smooth the edges to get a more natural looking composite. Usually a 1 pixel width will work, but you can always increase to 2 if needed.

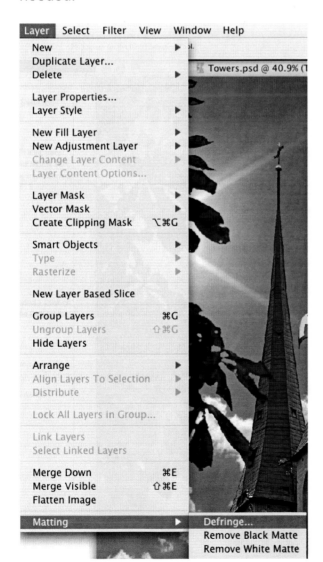

33. Activate the Towers layer.

34. **LAYER > MATTING > DEFRINGE**.

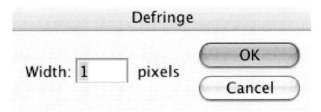

35. Make sure **"1" is in the WIDTH** name field.

36. Click **OK**.

37. **File > Save.**

Variations

The Variations Adjustment command allows you to globally correct color via thumbnails. It is not the most accurate way to adjust color, but it allows you to quickly adjust colors.

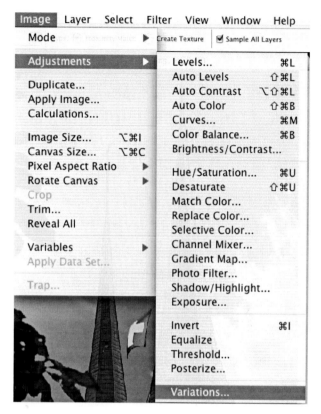

38. On the Towers Layer, **IMAGE > ADJUSTMENTS > VARIATIONS**.

39. You will see the Variations Dialog Box with thumbnails of the Towers layer.

40. Experiment with clicking on a color thumbnail to add color to the original. If you add too much color, click back on the thumbnail that is named "Original" and it will revert back to the original image.

41. When you get the Towers the color you wish, click the OK button.

42. FILE > SAVE.

Your finished document should look similar to the below image.

You may close the document.

Automation

Actions and Droplets come under Automation in Adobe Photoshop®. Actions allow you to record and save effects that you will repeat time after time to your images. This saves you from having to recreate the effect over and over again. You can run the Action as a Batch which will allow you to run the action on multiple images and save to a separate folder. Droplets are created from an Action. It is represented as an icon saved on your desktop for easy access.

You do not have to be in Photoshop to use the Droplet. Simply drag the image file on top of the Droplet on your desktop and the action will run.

Actions

Actions do not work well for some effects. Selections of items in a photo, for example, will not be the same in one photo as another. Brush strokes or any other manual tools will not work well either. General effects or auto adjustments that are not selection or image specific work best.

43. Open > Ferns.jpg.

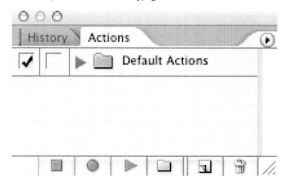

44. Fit on Screen.

45. Click on the Actions Palette Tab next to the History Palette Tab to bring the Actions Palette to the front.

46. You will see a folder in the Actions Palette named "Default Actions" that comes installed with Photoshop.

The menu below are the description of the icons you will use when creating Actions.

   1.   2.   3.   4.   5.   6.

     1. Stop playing or recording.
     2. Begin recording.
     3. Play the action.
     4. Create a new set of actions.
     5. Create a new action.

In order to create your own actions you must first create a folder for your actions.

47. In the Actions Palette, click on the **FOLDER** at the bottom of the palette to create a new set of actions folder.

48. In the Dialog Box that appears, type in "My Actions" to name the New Set.

49. Click OK.

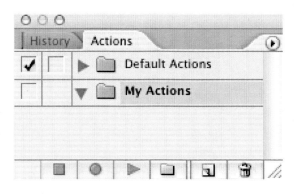

50. In the Actions Palette, you will see the new set appear. The set is empty, however. You must now create a New Action.

51. Click on the **NEW ACTION ICON** at the bottom of the Actions Palette.

New Action

Name: Output Image

Set: My Actions

Function Key: None ☐ Shift ☐ Command

Color: ☐ None

Record

Cancel

52. In the Name field, type in "Output Image."

53. Click the **RECORD BUTTON**.

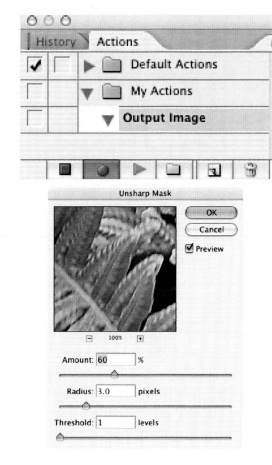

54. Everything you do to the image will now be recorded until you hit the STOP Icon in the Actions Palette.

55. The **Record Button** turns red in the Actions Palette indicating that you are recording. You also see the New Action (Output Image) listed as a subgroup of the My Actions Set.

You will begin creating the action.

56. **FILTER > SHARPEN > UNSHARP MASK.**

57. **Enter:**

> **Amount: 60**
>
> **Radius: 3.0**
>
> **Threshold: 1**

58. Click OK.

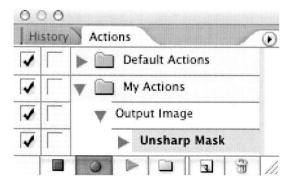

59. You can see the Unsharp Mask command in the Actions Palette appear.

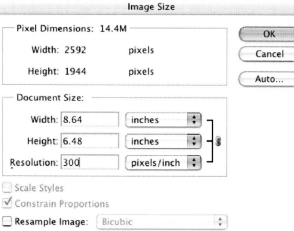

60. IMAGE > IMAGE SIZE.

61. The image needs a resolution of 300 ppi. The resolution of the image is 180 ppi.

62. **UNCHECK** the **RESAMPLE IMAGE** box and type in **300** in the **RESOLUTION** field.

63. Click **OK**.

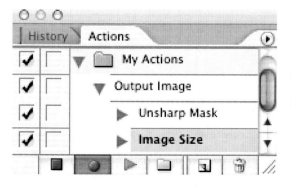

64. You can see the Image Size command in your Actions Palette.

65. **IMAGE > ADJUSTMENTS > AUTO LEVELS**.

66. **IMAGE > ADJUSTMENTS > AUTO COLOR**.

67. The color is not correct using this command. You will need to undo this part of your recording.

68. In the Actions Palette, click the **STOP** Button ▪ .

69. Drag the **last "LEVELS" action in the Actions Palette to the TRASH CAN ON THE ACTIONS PALETTE** to delete the last step.

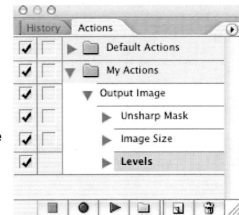

70. **FILE > REVERT** (to revert the image to its original state).

71. In the **Actions Palette, click on the Action "Output Image."**

72. Click on the **PLAY** ▶ button in the Actions Palette to play the action.

73. Click on the last action in the Actions Palette (**LEVELS**).

74. Click on the **RECORD BUTTON** ⦿ to begin recording.

75. **IMAGE > ADJUSTMENTS > AUTO CONTRAST**.

76. Another LEVELS appears in the Actions Palette.

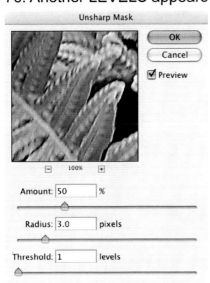

77. FILTER > SHARPEN > UNSHARP MASK (to sharpen one last time before output).

78. **Enter:**

Amount: 50

Radius: 3.0

Threshold: 1

79. Click **OK**.

80. IMAGE > MODE > CMYK (to convert color modes before final output to print).

81. FILE > SAVE AS .

82. CHANGE THE FILE FORMAT TO A **.TIFF format.**

83. CLICK the **Save** Button.

84. Click the OK button.

85. Click on the STOP button on the Actions Palette.

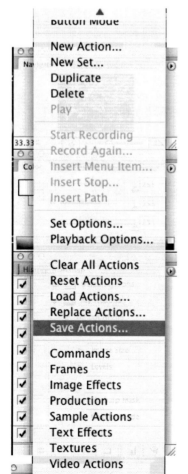

86. You must save the SET to keep your actions.

87. Click on the **MY ACTIONS folder** in your Actions Palette.

88. Click and hold the **FLYOUT BUTTON** on the Actions Palette to get **SAVE ACTIONS**.

89. In the SAVE ACTIONS dialog box, navigate to your desktop to save your actions.

90. Click **Save**.

91. Click on "Output Image" action in the Actions Palette.

92. **Open > Rocky Beach.jpg**

93. Click the **PLAY BUTTON** ▶ on the Actions Palette.

94. You see it go through the action, but you will not see the image change until the action is finished.

Creating a Droplet

As stated previously, a **DROPLET** is a miniature application composed of an action. It creates an icon on your desktop. You then can drag and drop images onto the icon without having Photoshop open. It opens Photoshop and runs the action.

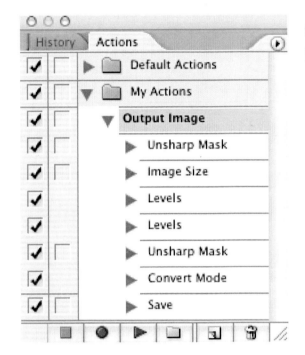

95. Make sure that , "**OUTPUT IMAGE**" is activated in your Actions Palette.

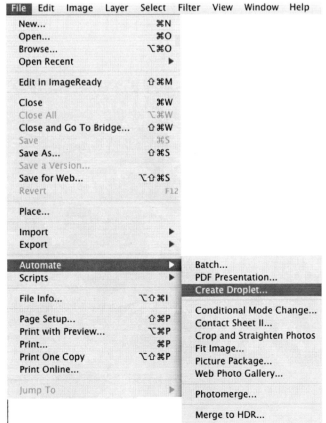

96. Go under **FILE > AUTOMATE > CREATE DROPLET**.

97. In the Dialog Box that appears, click the "CHOOSE" button to **choose the Desktop** for the Droplet Icon.

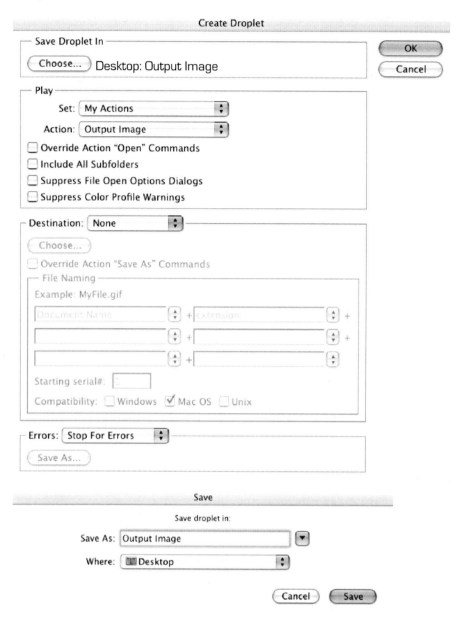

98. You also have a choice for DESTINATION. If you want to save your images to a folder, choose folder under this option.

99. Click OK.

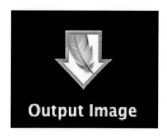

100. An icon will appear on your desktop.

101. Click on your Desktop.

102. Find a photo in a folder and drag and drop onto the Output Image Droplet icon on your desktop.

103. Close all images that are open in Photoshop.

Layer Comps

Layer Comps make it possible to have different options available within one file. For example, you might want to add a layer for one version of a composite, but other times, you may not want to see that version. This is convenient if you were showing a client different versions of the same composite so the client sees the options available.

104. Open > Shutter.psd.

105. Go under WINDOW > LAYER COMPS.

106. Drag the Layer Comps Tab to bring it out onto the Desktop.

107. Click the **NEW LAYER COMP** 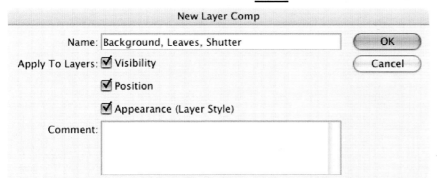 button in the Layer Comps Palette.

108. In the name field of the dialog box, type in: Leaves, Background, Shutter. Make sure that Visibility, Position and Appearance are checked.

109. Click the OK button.

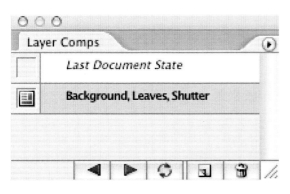

110. The Layer Comps Palette reflects the new Layer Comp.

112. In the Layers Palette, turn the Leaves layer off.

113. Click the **NEW LAYER COMP** button in the Layer Comps Palette.

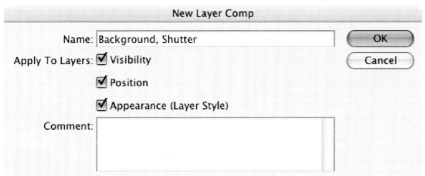

114. Type in Background, Shutter in the dialog box that appears.

115. Click OK.

116. Turn the Leaves Layer back on.

117. Choose **OVERLAY** as the Layer Blending Mode..

118. Click on the **NEW LAYER COMP ICON** and type in the dialog box: Background, **Leaves Overlay**, Shutter.

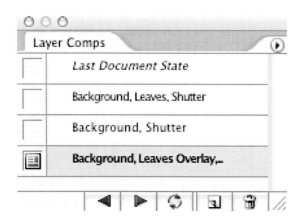

119. The Layer Comps Palette reflects the three versions of the document.

120. Click on the "**BACKGROUND, LEAVES SHUTTER**" Layer Comp to see that version.

121. Click on the "**BACKGROUND, SHUTTER**" to see that version of the composite.

122. **File > Save As > Layer Comp.psd**.

You may close the document.

Clipping Masks

You used Clipping Masks earlier. It allows you to combine two layers together with the bottom layer showing through the top (in the Surrealism Workshop). Here you will replace an area with a pattern to change the appearance.

123. Open > Clown.jpg

124. Open > Gingham.jpg.

125. Using the **MOVE TOOL, drag the Gingham image into the Clown image**.

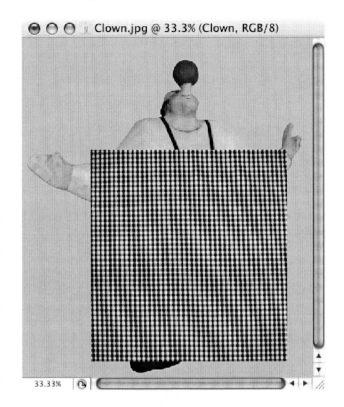

126. Position the Gingham over the pants of the Clown.

127. Rename Layer 1 to **Gingham**.

128. Rename *Background* to **Clown**.

129. You may close the Gingham document.

130. **File > Save As > Clipping Mask.PSD**.

131. Turn off the Gingham Layer to hide the layer.

132. Using the **Pen Tool (and the PATHS OPTION), trace the blue stripes in the pants of the Clown.** Remember to click and drag the Pen Tool to create a curved path. Use your OPTION KEY to change direction.

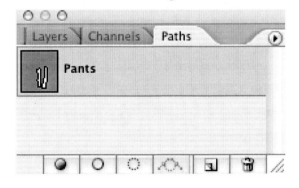

133. Save the Path as "**Pants**."

134. **LOAD the PATH as a SELECTION.**

135. **LAYER > NEW > LAYER VIA COPY (Command + J) or (Control + J).**

136. Go to the Layers Palette.

137. Name the new layer "Pants."

138. **HOLD THE OPTION / ALT KEY AND CLICK ON THE LINE BETWEEN THE GINGHAM LAYER AND THE PANTS LAYER** to make a Clipping Mask.

140. In the Layers Palette, you can see the Gingham Layer indented, showing the Clipping Mask.

141. Activate the Gingham Layer.

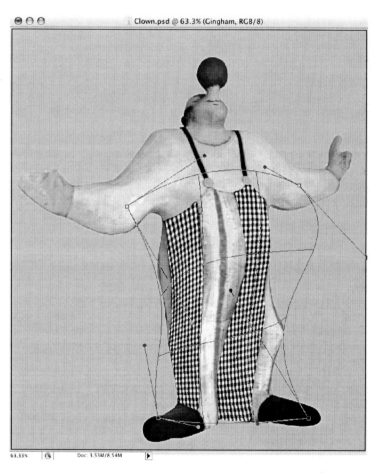

142. **EDIT >TRANSFORM > WARP**. This will warp the gingham to conform to the body of the Clown (IMAGE WARP).

143. Pull the corner handles of the **WARP TRANSFORMATION** to give a wrap-around effect.

144. Hit the **RETURN /ENTER KEY** when you have finished warping to make the transformation take effect.

145. Use the **BURN TOOL** (under the DODGE TOOL) to darken the left gingham stripe. Make sure you have a large enough Brush size).

146. FILE > SAVE AS > Gingham Clown.PSD.

Saving for the Web

When you are planning to take an image to the web, you need to make sure you optimize the JPEG first. In Photoshop there is a "SAVE FOR WEB" command. First you will need to **FLATTEN** the document.

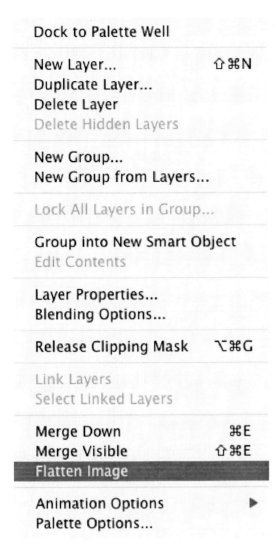

Dock to Palette Well

New Layer... ⇧⌘N
Duplicate Layer...
Delete Layer
Delete Hidden Layers

New Group...
New Group from Layers...

Lock All Layers in Group...

Group into New Smart Object
Edit Contents

Layer Properties...
Blending Options...

Release Clipping Mask ⌥⌘G

Link Layers
Select Linked Layers

Merge Down ⌘E
Merge Visible ⇧⌘E
Flatten Image

Animation Options ▶
Palette Options...

147. In the Layers Palette of the Gingham Clown document, click on the flyout arrow and choose FLATTEN IMAGE.

148. The Layers combine into one layer.

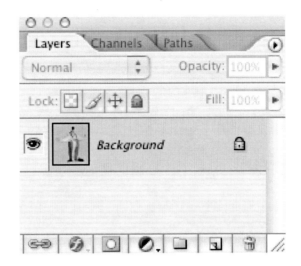

149. File > SAVE FOR WEB.

150. In the bottom left corner, change the viewing percentage to 25%.

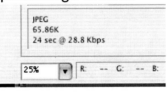

151. Choose the **4-Up** Tab at the top.

152. Choose **JPEG** from FILE FORMAT.

153. Choose **JPEG HIGH** from Compression Quality.

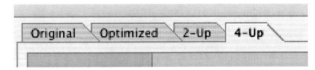

154. Click on the bottom left thumbnail and choose "GIF" to see the difference in the file size.

155. Click on the top right thumbnail to select it.

156. Make sure the settings on the left appear in the fields.

157. Once you have chosen your optimized settings, click the SAVE button to open the **SAVE OPTIMIZED AS** dialog box.

158. Navigate to your desktop folder to save the file.

Saving with a Transparent Background for the Web

In order to save an image with a transparent background for the web, you need to save the image as a GIF. First, you need to get rid of the background.

159. Double-click the background layer of the Gingham Clown to convert the *Background* into a layer. Name the layer "**Clown**."

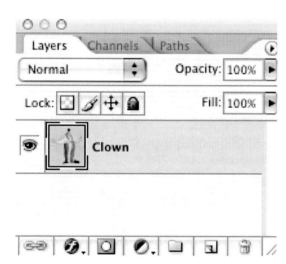

160. Using the **MAGIC WAND**, select the yellow background of the Gingham Clown.

161. **HIT THE DELETE KEY TO DELETE THE BACKGROUND**.

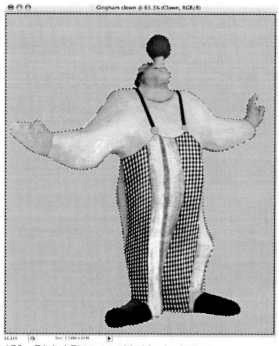
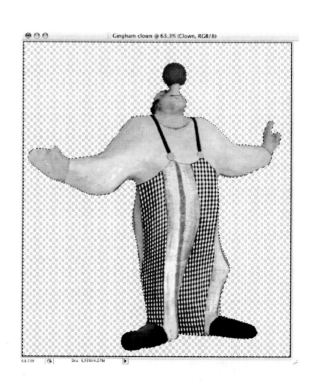

162. **Deselect**.

163. **FILE > SAVE FOR WEB**.

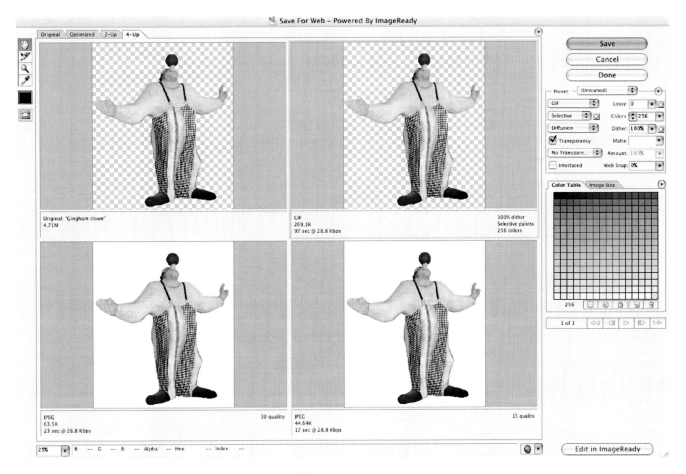

164. Enter 25% in the Zoom Percentage Box.

165. Click the top right thumbnail.

166. Change the file format to GIF.

167. Click the SAVE BUTTON.

168. Navigate to your Desktop Folder to save. The Clown will retain its transparent background when saving in a GIF format.

169. File > Close.

You have completed this tutorial.

Remember to drag your desktop folder to your USB Flash Drive after you've completed this tutorial OR BURN TO A CD.

APPENDIX

Common Photoshop Keyboard Shortcuts

	Mac	**Windows**
New	Cmd + N	Ctrl +N
Open	Cmd + O	Ctrl + O
Revert to Saved	F12	F12
Save	Cmd + S	Ctrl + S
Close	Cmd + W	Ctrl + W
Quit	Cmd + Q	Ctrl + Q
Undo	Cmd + Z	Ctrl + Z
Copy	Cmd + C	Ctrl + C
Cut	Cmd + X	Ctrl + X
Paste	Cmd + V	Ctrl + V
Paste Into	Cmd + Shift + V	Ctrl + Shift + V
Fit on Screen	Cmd + 0	Ctrl + 0
Select All	Cmd + A	Ctrl + A
Deselect	Cmd + D	Ctrl + D
Inverse	Cmd + Shift + I	Ctrl + Shift + I
Feather	Cmd + Option + D	Ctrl + Alt + D
Nudge	Arrow Key	Arrow Key
New Layer	Cmd + Shift + N	Ctrl + Shift + N
Layer Via Copy	Cmd + J	Ctrl + J
Layer Via Cut	Cmd + Shift + J	Ctrl + Shift + J
Merge Down (Layer)	Cmd + E	Ctrl + E
Merge Visible (Layers)	Cmd + Shift + E	Ctrl + Shift + E
Clipping Mask	Cmd + G	Ctrl + G
Release Clipping Mask	Cmd + Shift + G	Ctrl + Shift + G
Quick Mask	Q	Q
Free Transform	Cmd + T	Ctrl + T
Increase Brush Size	]	]
Decrease Brush Size	[	[
Move Tool	V	V
Lasso	L	L
Magic Wand	W	W
Clone Stamp	S	S
Eraser	E	E

	Mac	**Windows**
Healing Brush	J	J
Gradient	G	G
Brush	B	B
Hand	H	H
Hand	Hold Spacebar	Hold Spacebar
Pen	P	P
Zoom	Z	Z
Marquee	M	M
Type	T	T
Add to Selection	Shift + Click	Shift + Click
Subtract From Selection	Option + Click	Alt + Click
Zoom In	Cmd +	Ctrl +
Zoom Out	Cmd -	Ctrl -
Print	Cmd + P	Ctrl + P